Walk
Sleep
Repeat

Stephen Reynolds

Illustrations by Mark Reynolds

ISBN: 978-0-244-08656-5

PublishNation
www.publishnation.co.uk

Acknowledgements: (in no particular order)
Tasha, my folks and step-folks, Bruv & Tom, my lovely grandparents and all the family and friends who have supported and encouraged me in my foolhardy attempts to give this writing malarkey a go. Last but not least all of the wonderful folks I met along the West Highland Way that helped to make the hike so memorable.

Special Thanks: To Teddy – My editor, proof reader and chief reality enforcer. My baby bruv Mark for the utterly amazing artwork and Dan for the free legal advice.

Contents

Walk
Sleep
Repeat

MILNGAVIE

DRYMEN

ROWARDENNAN

CRAINLARICH

BRIDGE OF ORCHY

KINLOCHLEVIN

FORT WILLIAM

Prologue

At some point towards the end of summer a couple of years ago I was in something of a funk. An accumulation of stress, poor health and lack of exercise had manifested themselves as a prolonged period of insomnia. I was a miserable and out-of-shape zombie wandering aimlessly through the scrapheap of life, looking for a place to lie down amongst the wreckage... Without a pillow... Or any pyjamas... or... slippers? Oy, this metaphor is going nowhere. Bad start. Right. Come on, Reynolds. Focus, you need to regain control of this paragraph... Which - in itself - is *kind of* a metaphor for my predicament at that time. Clever... Is it? Maybe not. Anyway - the point being - it was a low point. Then one bleary-eyed morning I decided to go for a walk. I ended up walking for the entire day and my problems seemed to temporarily melt away. I then hobbled home exhausted and slept for a solid twelve hours. The weeks and months that followed were the glorious discovery of a life-changing passion. Long-distance hiking had, to put it somewhat grandiosely and in doing so probably overstate the thing a touch, saved my life. I was spending an increasingly large proportion of my spare time exploring the trails and footpaths of our green and pleasant land and feeling a good deal better for it with each and every step.

Eventually this led me to embark on the adventure of a lifetime by walking the UK's longest National Trail: the 630-mile-long South West Coast Path. But that's another story. Actually, it literally is another story, as I wrote a book about it. It was an international smash-hit (I sold one copy in Japan...

Thanks Gav), not to mention critically acclaimed (my mum called it 'very nice'). So - if you haven't done so already - you should probably go and read it now. Have you finished? What did you think? Droned on a bit, eh? A tendency to branch off when you least expected it and waffle on about unrelated subjects. I mean to say, what on Earth was all that stuff about golf? I know lots of golfers and they're lovely people. Mostly... By and large... Well at worst they're a mixed bunch. In any case, you'll be pleased to hear that there'll be none of that nonsense this time round. I've grown; matured as an author. There'll be none of that difficult second album syndrome either. Quite the opposite as it happens; I'm expecting this to be my chef-d'oeuvre (see - look at the clever words I'm using - growth *and* maturity). In fact, to be honest with you, dear reader, I also fully expect to have achieved national treasure status by the time you finish reading this book. Right then, where were we? Oh yes, so now that you've all read the trailblazing debut let's bring you up to speed with what's been going on since then.

My life has very much become a before and after affair, as far as walking the Coast Path goes. Since returning to normality I have boldly set about reshaping said normality, so as to better suit the new and improved S. Reynolds. That perhaps makes it sound a *tiny* bit more dramatic than it may actually be. Basically, I've gone part-time at work so that I can spend more time walking. Somewhere in the region of 50 per cent of my waking life is now spent on the trail. The result of which is an infinitely happier and equally infinitely poorer S. Reynolds. Can something be equally infinite? Doesn't sound right does it? Doesn't matter, what does matter though - as far as you're concerned – is that this has given me the opportunity to walk a variety of other long-distance trails. These have included the Coleridge Way, the Cotswolds Way, the Mendip Way and the Two Moors Way, to name but a few. Some have been completed in one go but most a few days at a time, using my new-found freedom vis-à-vis the reduced employment hours. As well as the weekends, every Monday and Tuesday are now given over exclusively to the wondrous isolation of the long-distance hike. The one you're going to hear about though is the one I consider to be my second real adventure. A week in bonny Scotland hiking the beautiful West Highland Way.

The following is written using notes I've taken at the end of each day's walking, as well as from memory. As the big four-zero looms ever closer I'm conscious that the old memory may not be quite what it once was. Or maybe it is, I forget. In any case, you'll forgive me I'm sure, the odd factual inaccuracy as we embark together on one of the UK's most striking and memorable trails. Nothing major you understand but I may, from time to time, put a hill in slightly the wrong place... That kind of thing.

17th July 2017: The Preamble

Tasha rolls over in bed and without opening her eyes mumbles, 'Try not to get lost.' She's resumed snoring a few seconds later. I should probably make it clear at this point that Tasha is my partner... Without that knowledge this scene has a very different feel to it. For a start, if she's not my partner then what am I doing in the bedroom of a young(ish) lady on the very morning that I'm meant to be heading off to Scotland? I wouldn't want you to get the wrong impression regards your narrator from the get-go. Right then, emotional goodbyes duly dispensed with, I proceed with childlike excitement to get myself dressed and ready for the off. I sling the trusted old backpack over the shoulders and march off into the sunset... Or rather sunrise... Well no, actually it isn't that either as it's already daylight... I leave the house.

I'm only five minutes down the road when I remark to myself; 'Blimey! This backpack is quite heavy.' I had decided a few weeks prior that I didn't need to bother practicing walking with the full-sized and fully packed backpack in advance of this trip, instead continuing to use the good old day pack for my weekly adventures. I mean I'm an experienced hiker nowadays after all. I've carried the thing around the whole south west coast of England. I know my own strength thank you very much and I like to think that I have a pretty good handle on what I need to take along on a hike such as this... So, let's call that mistake number one of the trip shall we, dear reader? By the time I arrive at Bristol Temple Meads train station my shoulders are aching but my excitement regards what lies ahead is positively palpable. An enthusiasm that is already being put to the test a mere 30 minutes into the journey, as the prospect of a further eight hours sat on the train fully dawns on me.

You may be thinking to yourself at this point that travelling from Bristol to Milngavie (where the trail begins) by train is a strange choice. Well, I must say that this reflects badly on you, in my humble opinion. I suppose you assume that just because a chap has a crippling fear of flying it means he can't be a brave and handsome Indiana Jones-type explorer, do you? Well shame on you, dear reader... And dash it all, I feel a pang of sorrow for you for harbouring such a blinkered world view. Right then, where were we? Oh yes, long train journey. I decide to use the time wisely by reading through the guidebook for the trail. This succeeds in keeping the excitement going and staving off the boredom admirably.

The West Highland Way is roughly 100 miles long and takes in some of the most stunning scenery in the UK. Although it begins not far from the bustling city of Glasgow, it passes through some of the most remote stretches of wilderness a walker can hope to experience on these shores. The photographs in the guidebook are hairs-standing-up-on-the-back-of-the-neck beautiful. Dramatic and rugged landscapes filled with grand imposing mountains and shimmering reflective lochs. The potential for spotting all manner of wildlife is tantalising as well. From Highland cows to stags and even wildcats. Of particular interest to yours truly is the prospect of seeing a golden eagle. Since finding a passion for hiking I've become borderline obsessed with the birds of prey that call this island home. On my home turf in the south west of England I regularly see kestrels, sparrowhawks and (slightly less regularly) peregrines. My favourite though is undoubtedly the buzzard. I've spent countless hours gazing up at this shy yet majestic creature as it glides, hovers, swoops and dives in search of prey. The prospect therefore of catching sight of the comparatively giant golden eagle has seen me counting down the days and hours to the start of this trip.

Above all else though, I'm looking forward to rediscovering the freedom of the long-distance trail. The shedding of all of life's unwanted distractions until your world is stripped back to leave you only with what really matters: Walk. Sleep. Repeat. Once I've looked at all the pictures and read the accompanying blurb I put the book away and glance at the time on my phone. Seven hours to go. Just as I'm beginning to lament my decision not to take the more expensive sleeper train, a man sits down on the seat directly across the aisle from me. He's about six foot four and at a guess roughly the same width ways. He's carrying several full-to-the-brim supermarket bags for life, which he positions all around him; taking up another seat and blocking the aisle. It's a hot mid-July day but he's wearing a grey suit that's a good few sizes too small for him and a large thick high-viz yellow safety workman's overcoat. A strong smell of tuna wafts over to me.

'I'm going all the way,' he says very loudly, looking in my direction.

'Oh right,' I reply, with a nervous smile. Seven hours of pretending to be asleep suddenly looming into view.

'Yes, all the way for me. Are you English?' he asks in the same booming voice.

'Yes, that's right.'

'Oh, you're in for a treat, Scotland's nice.' (Pauses) 'I like the train.' He smiles at me with genuine delight and I find that I'm unable to stop myself returning the grin.

Over the next seven hours we chat and snooze intermittently. The fellow's name is Liam and he's heading home to visit family in Glasgow. Despite talking for hours on end that's really all I ever find out about him. For the most part, he's providing me with a running commentary of our journey.

'Pulling into Birmingham New Street now... Just leaving Carlisle now. 70,000 people live in Carlisle... Here we are in Berwick-Upon-Tweed... There's the water on my left... We're going to be crossing the water... Now.' Always at a thumping volume that draws stares from the other passengers. Liam eats four full tins of tuna during the journey, offering me some at increasingly regular intervals, despite my continued polite rebuffs. He is a kind-hearted, thoroughly decent and fascinating chap and I feel more than a pang of shame regards the sense of dread that washed over me when he sat down beside me and the first clouds of brined fish flooded my nostrils. When we eventually arrive in Glasgow I say goodbye, shake him by the hand and wish him all the best before wandering off to find my connecting train to Milngavie.

The remainder of the journey passes uneventfully. The views from the window become increasingly picturesque as my excitement for the week ahead returns. Milngavie is pronounced 'Mill-guy' and is a pleasant enough town to host the start of the trail. A small non-descript shopping centre, a busy main road and rows and rows of (not-unattractive) period

8

housing. It has something of the feel of a commuter town about it, which I suppose it is, being so close to Glasgow. As I walk through it to find my hotel for the night I pass several nods to the West Highland Way in the colourful shop windows; from souvenir tea towels and t-shirts to commemorative flasks and sew-on badges. I also pass the striking granite obelisk that marks the start of the trail. I stop to take a photograph and send it to Tasha, my mum and stepdad Dennis, my dad (Pops) and stepmum Jane and my brother Mark and his partner Tom. AKA – those lucky few who will receive in excess of a thousand photographs via WhatsApp over the coming few days.

I'm booked into a Premier Inn for the night and once I've checked in and dumped the backpack, I head off in search of some dinner and liquid refreshment. I come across an initially enticing local pub – but as I approach it I notice that everyone stood outside of it looks like Begbie from Trainspotting – and I'm too scared to go inside. In the end, I bravely plump for the restaurant attached to my hotel and order the only vegetarian option on the menu. I've only very recently become a vegetarian and have found that, among other things, it certainly makes choosing your meal a good deal easier when eating out. After wolfing down some kind of tomato-pasta-thingy I order a single malt whisky on the rocks. I'm a pretty classy fellow, dear reader. It's probably best that you understand that about me from the kick-off. As I lie in bed later that evening, my excited anticipation is such that I decide to set my alarm for 6am. The sooner I'm on the trail the better.

DAY ONE

Drymen

Milngavie

Day 1: Milngavie to Drymen

Tantalising Glimpses, Turnip Pizzas & Dutch Cigars

Day one begins, as all good days should, with the difficult choice between a banana and a strawberry Weetabix breakfast drink. This is not a decision to be taken lightly as I'm sure you'll appreciate. One must judge the mood of the day correctly. Which is to say, if it's a strawberry kind of a day and you slurp down a banana without due consideration then you're potentially in all kinds of trouble. (Note: I am aware that you can also purchase chocolate or vanilla flavour Weetabix drinks... But I don't recognise these. Vanilla for breakfast? Absurd.) Of course, when we were last together, dear reader, the world knew nothing of the Weetabix drink. It was just the crazy reckless dream of those pioneering folk over at Weetabix HQ. It amazes me when I think back to all those days hiking that began with the laborious task of eating actual Weetabix. Pouring the milk, lifting the spoon, chewing... Unenlightened times. A thrill-seeking and fly-by-the-seat-of-the-pants explorer such as myself has no time for these quaint distractions. With a few more moments of careful deliberation I conclude it's definitely a strawberry kind of a day.

After washing, dressing and lacing up the trusty old boots I reach for the Avon Skin So Soft. As you'll no doubt be aware, the good people of Scotland are forced to go about their everyday lives whilst under constant threat of attack from a relentless and terrifying aggressor; to wit, the midge. Dastardly little blighters against whom one must obtain adequate protection if one is to survive. Alice Walker - a friend of ours who is an experienced hiker - stopped me in my tracks when I was naively considering buying a bottle of purpose-made midge repellent and insisted I instead use Avon Skin So Soft. (For those of you that failed to spot that... I'll spell it out: we have a friend who loves hiking and is actually named A. Walker... You can't make this stuff up people.) As the name suggests it's actually a beauty product but for those in the know it's apparently the best defence there is against the dreaded *Culicoides Impunctatus*. (Did you see that? That's Latin... Seriously it is. I ought to know, I just looked it up. It means midge. Growth *and* maturity.) Even the marines use it (or so I'm told). Safe in the knowledge that A. Walker is a dependable chum I duly apply generous amounts and make my slippery and shiny way out of the hotel.

The bright early morning sun is already emitting a sweltering heat as I make my way through the deserted streets back towards the obelisk and the official start of the trail. As is so often the case, the first few miles of the trail is a question of negotiating my way through an urban landscape in the quest to reach the wilderness. No matter how remote the trail, the start and end points must logically be reachable by public transport, which often means that some of the greatest walks out there both begin and finish unremarkably. Being a chipper fellow, I like to see this as in some way symbolic. The leaving behind of - and eventual returning to - the 'real world'. Toodle pip, civilization, you frightful old bore, see you on the other side.

The path initially runs alongside a stream before crossing underneath a main road as it weaves its way out of Milngavie. After a while the houses and the early morning hum of traffic are replaced by overhanging trees and the cheerful calls of the resident chaffinch. Just as I start to think that I may have at last left the town behind me a Lycra-clad chap out jogging passes by. As we nod our greetings I notice that he's wearing a t-shirt which says 'In America they call it survival. In South Africa we call it camping.' As well as being a mildly amusing aside this gets me thinking, oddly enough, about camping. My thoughts wander to the tent, roll matt and sleeping bag currently weighing down my pack and causing a degree of unwelcome chafing to the old shoulder region. It may shock you to hear, dear reader, that yours truly was on the receiving end of more than a little unsportsmanlike japery regards this very subject only recently. Upon reading of my heroic adventures walking the South West Coast Path some of my hitherto considered chums, indeed – if you can believe it - even the odd member of my own kith-and-kin, seemed to derive a good deal of amusement from the fact that I hauled all that weight around for 630-miles despite only actually camping a half dozen times. Well I assure you there'll be no such japery at the conclusion of *this* trail. We'll see who's laughing 100 or so miles from now shall we? Growth and maturity is what I'm saying to you. I mean... As you're already aware I stayed in a hotel last night... And now seems like as good a moment as any to put it out there that I will be staying in a hotel again tonight. But that's it... From then on, it's just me and the wilderness – man and nature. At one with the canvas. *'Out here in the fields, where I fight for my meals...'* Well you get the picture.

The path is now deep within rich, mixed woodland and the bright sunlight bounces through the branches to dapple the ground ahead of me with a kaleidoscope of greens. I'm once again beside a stream and the sound of gently flowing water is a welcome addition to the continued uplifting birdsong. This cheerful summertime stroll through the woodland continues for a mile or so before I reach a road that signals an end to the tree cover for the time being. My spirits are momentarily dampened by the site of the dreaded tarmac, but I've only gone a few steps along the road when a waymarker guides me across it and through a stile on the other side. I had always supposed that the symbol for all National Trails across the UK was the good old acorn, but here in Scotland the waymarkers are adorned with an image of the iconic Scottish thistle. This somehow adds to the sense adventure as it further cements the sensation of being a long way from home.

Through the stile; and the trail gives me the first fleeting glimpse of things to come. The merest sniff of Highland splendour. The view opens up and a tremendous feeling of limitless space briefly washes over me. The path winds downwards to cross a river as a vast tree-covered hill proudly dominates the vista. I stroll along a rocky path for a few minutes before turning a corner to be greeted by the sight of the first loch of the journey. Craigallian Loch is but a babe-in-arms when compared with some of those I'll encounter over the next few days. Yet, as it shimmers in the sunlight it is nevertheless a welcome sight as this early section of the trail seeks to establish its own character. The path takes me alongside the water and allows me time to watch contentedly as a dozen or so moorhens lazily drift across the calm surface of the loch.

I then enter the second woodland stretch of the day in the form an atmospheric conifer plantation. The clear blue sky and sparkling water are replaced by the spooky gloom particular to these types of plantations. At the risk of offending the purists I must confess to a love of walking through man-made woods such as this. I mean to say; obviously it lacks all the rich beauty of your bang-to-rights ancient forest. There's no tapestry of colour or buzz of life, no sense of history or evidence of nature's beautiful chaos. Yet, there is something else. Something that only the perfect rows of tall imposing trees, emitting their thick and all-consuming darkness, are able to evoke. A kind of other-worldliness that conjures up thoughts of

14

childhood nightmares and the boogie-man into the mind of even the pluckiest rambler.

This sensory revelling is over before it's really begun however, as the plantation abruptly ends and I'm thrust into the warm sunshine once more. After a few minutes I pass a collection of tumble-down wooden cabins on my left. As I look over the characterful, ramshackle structures I'm struck by their contrast to the mathematical uniformity of the conifers I've just left behind. Despite their undoubted charm and my own musings as to how wonderful it would be to live out here, I'm powerless to prevent my tiny warped mind from introducing a whiff of *Deliverance* into the scene. As the infamous banjo tune starts to play out in my head my pace quickens slightly. I immediately pass-by the second loch of the day; the even smaller Carbeth Loch. Just as this sight returns my mood to one of calm serenity the path unceremoniously plonks me out onto a busy road.

Whilst I fully appreciate that if you're intending to walk long distances on the British Isles then you're going to have to accept the odd stretch of tarmac along the way, I must confess to a twinge of annoyance every time a trail presents me with such a challenge. Indeed, it is with an almost accusatory tone that I reach for the guidebook to find out how long I can expect to be trudging alongside the sparse but speeding early morning commuters on this occasion. The official guidebook for the West Highland Way is written by a Mr... Well, now you see I'm never really sure what's the done thing regards including names, perhaps the fellow doesn't want to be in my book? Let's just call him Mr B. to be on the safe side. At this early stage of the hike the thing is already proving to be a worthwhile companion. As luck would have it Mr B. advises me that I'll only be enduring the roadside for a few more minutes. He also points out that rather than moaning about it I should probably glance to my right and appreciate the views of the impressive Campsie Fells. Duly noted, Mr B. old boy.

In any case, I soon reach the waymarker that points to pastures new. I'm now on a pleasant enough farm track crossing through lush green fields as herds of cows merrily graze away in the increasing heat of the July sun. The track ends abruptly at the border of a field and I clamber over a stile to survey what lies beyond. I'm suddenly frozen where I stand as the eyes widen and the dutiful jaw accordingly drops. I check behind me to verify the presence of a humble stile, rather than some kind of magical portal to another dimension. I've been instantly transported from quaint farmland to remote Highland drama. The picture ahead of me consists of two large hills that frame a spectacular view of magnificent far-away mountains. The first mountains I've seen on this trip and the sight is enough to send a ruddy good tingle up the old spine. I pause for a minute and even reach for the phone to take a photograph. As if to add a finishing touch to the grandeur of the scene I catch sight of the first bird of prey of the trip, gliding serenely overhead. It's too small to be a buzzard and it's not a kestrel either. I stare up at it through the glare of the sun but I'm unable to identify it before it passes by. I make a mental note to consult those reliable and informative folks over at the internet later today.

The path itself has also adopted a more rugged Highland mentality as it weaves its rocky way through the landscape. I'm in seventh heaven as I plough onwards through the undulating terrain. After a half a mile or so I spy a striking set of large boulders in the distance. They are too uniformly placed to be a natural occurrence. I consult Mr B. to be advised that these are the Dumgoyach Standing Stones; possibly the remains of the entrance to an ancient tomb. Behind them proudly stands the tree-covered Dumgoyach Hill which slowly looms into ever closer view as the path winds its way around it.

I'm reminded of many a walk across windswept Exmoor with my Pops as I continue to soak up the stunningly desolate surroundings. My Pops is the quintessential Exmoor man, blessed with a natural sense of direction (which he has, somewhat selfishly, failed to pass on through the genes to his hapless first-born). I've lost count of the times we've been following a forgotten but still well-defined single-file track through the vast open moorland, open to the all-to-often harsh and unforgiving elements, only for him to suddenly veer off course and start striding confidently off in another direction.

'Er... I think it's this way, Pops.'

'No, no, this way's better.'

We're usually accompanied by his faithful sheepdog Tiny, and it's at this point that Tiny and I glance knowingly at each other before, with a mutual shrug of the shoulders, following him blindly into the empty wilderness with tails wagging. Sure enough our 'off-piste' diversion will always yield something over and above the tried and tested pathway and has never yet failed to get us home.

I'm awoken from my daydreams by another stile, set into an attractive dry-stone wall. To my slight disappointment this brings about yet another abrupt change of landscape. I'm plunged back into the sprawling farmland scenery of a few miles prior. It's as though the first day of the trail had borrowed a patch of land from a later section – so as to provide a tantalising taste of what's in store for the anticipatory walker. At least I hope that's the case, because as pleasant as the open farmland strolling undoubtedly is, I'm craving the remote wilderness of the Highlands that the dramatic photographs displayed in Mr B.'s pages have promised me. I pass fields dotted with freshly shorn sheep eyeing me with blasé indifference, before arriving at a wooden footbridge that crosses a fast-flowing river. I pause here for a few minutes to watch the water stream by underneath me and give my shoulders a breather, by taking the opportunity to sling off the cursed backpack.

Once suitably invigorated I forge bravely ahead, going where no man has gone b… Well no not quite, but I am starting to take note of the fact that I've yet to pass a fellow rambler. I do have a tendency to kick off unpalatably early in the morning; such is my infantile excitement to be 'on the trail' once more. Yet, I had supposed I'd have had a few encounters by now, on a sunny July morning such as this. As I ponder this I come to a waymarker that signals I'm to turn left onto a wide country lane. It bears all the tell-tale hallmarks of a former railway line with its straight, flat surface carving its way through the landscape and off into the distance. The walking is easy as I stroll on leisurely, passing between hills on either side of me and briefly through more patches of woodland.

Eventually I pass the fine sight of Glengoyne distillery on my right. Purveyors of finest single malt whisky. This coaxes the old salivary glands from their slumber and into action. Traditionally of course, I'm a straight-up no-nonsense ale drinker. A shoot-from-the-hip adventurer with simple tastes. Yet, as part of my thorough preparations for this trip, I considered it only sporting to acquire a taste for this most cultured of Scottish mainstays. One must do one's utmost to embrace the local customs – it's only right and proper. To the same respectful end, I also intend to swig down more than a few litres of Irn-Bru and come away with at least a basic understanding of what constitutes a neep and/or a tattie by the end of this trip.

With thoughts of fine whisky still swirling around the old noggin the path crosses a road and the tempting sight of an attractive old pub looms into view. You'll be pleased to hear though, dear reader, that the trusty old self-discipline shows up in the nick of time and politely points out that a pre-lunch tipple on day one of the journey would not be an astute decision. I begrudgingly accept this assertion and trudge onwards. The lane passes through acres of pleasant farmland, a not-so-pleasant sewage works and continued patches of woodland whilst all the while remaining flat and easy-going.

At one point I finally get my first sighting of some fellow walkers as I pass a row of tents adorning the side of the lane. Scotland's open access policy allows for wild camping all throughout the trail. A fact which succeeds in encouraging even the most reluctant of campers (such as yours truly) to embrace the notion of nights under the canvas. The idea of pitching where you please and spending a night in the remote wilderness has plenty of the romanticism about it. At one with nature and all that. These particular campers are clearly only just rising to seize the day as I pass them by. They're emerging bleary-eyed from their tents with saucepans in one hand and toothbrushes in the other. I'm sorry to report that my chipper calls of 'Good morning to you!' are met with something closer to confusion and/or irritation than the plucky comradeship with which they're delivered.

I must confess that after a little while longer the (apparently infinite) country lane is starting to lose some of its peaceful easy-going vibe and beginning to feel like something more akin to a relentless slog. Just as my spirits begin to waver however, I'm treated to the sight of three graceful deer leaping past enthusiastically in the distance. This is one of those sights that simply never get old. As I've now given over a large proportion of my day-to-day life to wandering the countryside, I'm lucky enough to catch sight of wildlife like this on an at least semi-regular basis. Yet, as with the buzzards and kestrels, any spotting of these flighty and timid creatures evokes in me the same sense of elusive wonder and novelty as it did the first time. The pleasure gained from this encounter carries me through the remaining miles of the country lane until I eventually come to another bridge that signifies its conclusion.

My relief at this is short-lived however; as it quickly becomes apparent that the path is leaving the lane only to immediately join a road. Initially though, this proves to be pleasingly picturesque as I stroll downwards to cross another river in the hamlet of Gartness. Here I find an impressive waterfall set amongst sandstone rocks, with endlessly cascading water that sparkles brilliantly in the bright sunlight. I decide this is a good spot for an early lunch and plonk myself down facing the falls. I delve into the pack for my daily rations. Now, you may have heard rumour, dear reader, that my culinary decision-making when embarking on heroic explorations such as this leaves something to be desired. I'm happy to confirm therefore, that this is nonsense. Pure fiction created and spread by dishonourable sourpusses. Up until very recently I've been fuelled exclusively on Mars Bars and salami but, due to my recent switch to vegetarianism and continuing the theme of growth and maturity, I can now report that I'll be luncheoning on Mars Bars and processed stringy cheese snacks for the duration. So - you see - perfectly proper and above board and nothing remotely of any interest or concern. I'm glad to have cleared that up.

Afternoon

After consuming my tasty, stringy savoury and my nougaty sweet, I head off for what Mr B. advises me will be a relatively short jaunt to the final destination for the day; the village of Drymen. The heat has cranked up a notch in the last hour or so and I start to perspire as the sun beats relentlessly down on me. To add to this, the path, although still following the road, is beginning to climb and fall with more frequency. A second disused railway line runs alongside the road for a spell before veering off as the path continues, overlooking a picture-postcard valley complete with stream and colourful flora. As the road climbs once more, I get one last sight of the Campsie Hills in the far distance. I make my sweaty way onwards as the road starts to become busier the closer I get to Drymen. In amongst the odd speeding car there seems to be an inexhaustible number of cyclists rushing past. I smile and say good morning more times in a one mile stretch than I have done in possibly the whole of the last year.

I eventually get to leave the road for a brief spell in order to cross a pleasingly muddy field, which also contains therein the first Highland cows of the trail. These huge shaggy bovines with their big flat faces and curved horns are a joy to behold in their natural habitat. This gushing appreciation clearly isn't mutually felt however as they barely look up from their grazing whilst I squelch my clumsy and undignified way through the mud. I then reach the edge of the field and another road. The trail turns right but I go left, to follow the road into Drymen – today's final destination. As I'm walking along the pavement and houses begin to appear, I glance at my phone to discover it's only just turned 1pm. At twelve miles, today's walk is the shortest that I have planned but it nevertheless feels a bit odd to be ending the day's hike so early. I think back over the walk. It's been the quintessential first day really. Relatively unchallenging with occasional glimpses of the spectacular. All very pleasant but with a lingering feeling that things still haven't really got going.

My first impressions of Drymen, as I wander through it towards my hotel for the night, are of a pleasant village built around an attractive central square. The square consists of a large patch of grass circled by a lane, which is in turn adorned with welcoming pubs and restaurants. These include the Clachan pub, which claims to be the oldest in Scotland and to have links back to Rob Roy himself. It only seems right and proper therefore to pencil in a visit for later this evening... For cultural purposes obviously. I continue down one of the side roads past a post office and numerous tiny cafés and shops. Eventually I arrive at my digs for the night, check in at reception and make my way through the rabbit warren of a building to my room.

After taking a bath and writing up some notes I decide to call Tasha and my folks in turn. I talk through the day with each of them, tailoring the story slightly in each case to suit the listener. In my mum's version of the day I make sure to emphasize how safe and friendly everything is. A well signposted stroll in clean pants with a hearty meal waiting for me at the finish line. And definitely no talking to strangers. Failure to do this may well result in mother dearest, with a beleaguered Dennis in tow, jumping on the first flight up here with a bag of sandwiches and some wet wipes. In Pop's version of events I focus on the short stretch of true Highland walking early on, as he shares my love of the wilderness. I'm careful to withhold information regards how much money I'm wasting on fancy hotels whilst continuing to lug my camping equipment around on my back. I'm also causing some degree of alarm by setting up a joint WhatsApp group with both him and Jane in order to share photographs of the hike – the idea that all three of us can talk at once being construed as some kind of voodoo black magic by the pair of them. Lastly, in Tasha's version of events I'm basically Indiana Jones. Heroically swashbuckling my way through an unforgiving and desolate landscape. Fighting fierce birds of prey and rabid, vicious Highland cows along the way. My rippling torso glistens with perspiration as I make increasingly hilarious wisecracks whilst escaping each life-threatening scenario.

Eventually, after failing miserably to identify the bird of prey I saw earlier, I don the glad rags (to wit: Carter USM t-shirt, shorts and a fresh shiny layer of Avon Skin So Soft) and head out to paint Drymen red. I decide to start with a tipple at the hotel bar. I'm presented with a bottle of heather ale. An intriguing and tasty offering from a local Scottish brewery. Once dispatched I make my way back up to the central square in search of a place to eat. I'm taken aback to find the sleepy village has been completely overrun by fellow ramblers. The central patch of grass is packed with exhausted bodies collapsed beside discarded backpacks and muddy boots. The tables outside the pubs that encircle the square are equally full to bursting. Having barely seen a soul all day the scene is verging on the surreal. This is obviously the scheduled finishing time for stage one… For all those walkers that don't set off as absurdly early as yours truly. Amongst them I spy a few of the bleary-eyed folks I passed emerging from their tents earlier.

Slightly dumbfounded I make my way through the crowds to a restaurant with a blackboard out front advertising pizza. Despite the relatively early hour I'm lucky to get a table in the small bustling establishment. I barely glance at the menu before deciding on the turnip pizza. I mean to say, who wouldn't order a turnip pizza when presented with such an opportunity? When it arrives, it's a pizza with some bits of turnip on it. On reflection I'm not really sure what I expected it to be, dear reader, but I must confess to being a touch disappointed. Still, you live and learn. When next presented with the chance of a turnip pizza I will pause to peruse the rest of the menu before jumping in. It is a tasty pizza when all is said and done, so all's well that ends well.

Later that evening I'm sat at a table outside the oldest pub in Scotland. The bulk of the crowds have dispersed to their respective lodgings but the pub is still alive with the hum of conversation. I'm sipping on a whisky when a lady, maybe in her sixties, appears and asks if the seat next to me is free. She has a thick Dutch accent, blue trimmed glasses and a mass of curly grey hair. All of which is secondary to the fact that she is smoking a cigar the size of my arm. I've recently quit smoking and the glorious smell that she's emitting has caught my attention in much the same way that a shiny thing catches the attention of a curious magpie. She too is sipping at a whisky and as she sits down beside me I sense a kindred spirit.

'I thought Scotland is meant to be cold,' she says, pulling a face of mock exasperation and pretending to mop her brow.

'Haha, yes I know what you mean. It's a scorcher, eh?'

'A "scorcher?"'

'Sorry, I mean a hot day,' I reply. In truth I'm barely registering what she's saying as the intoxicating cigar smoke cascades around me. I have to summon all my strength to stop myself snatching it from her hand and making a mad run for it. We sit and chat for the next hour or so and I discover she is on a kind of touring holiday of Scotland. Stopping at various cities, attractions and landmarks. She's staying in Drymen tonight because she doesn't want to stay in the centre of Glasgow. I confess again that much of what she says is a blur to me. I'm busy focusing on inhaling as much of the cigar smoke as possible without looking too obvious. I do remember though that we discuss a long-distance hike in the Netherlands called Pieterpad, which she whole-heartedly recommends. I vow to look it up and eventually, when I've had my fill of second-hand smoke, we say our goodbyes and I head off back to my hotel.

Back in my room I consult Mr B. regards tomorrow's walk. This ends up yielding an untimely minor bombshell for your intrepid narrator. Upon closer inspection (i.e. actually bothering to read the guidebook) it turns out that climbing the UK's highest mountain; Ben Nevis at the end of the trail does not make up the last day of the hike as I had pre-supposed, but rather is in *addition* to the hike proper. Meaning it requires an extra day.

As my train ticket home is booked already this means I am either going to miss out on climbing Ben Nevis or have to drastically increase my daily mileage to finish the trail a day early. Let's call that mistake number two of the trip, dear reader. It's whilst pondering this conundrum that I eventually drift off into sleep.

DAY TWO

Rowardennan

Drymen

Day 2: Drymen to Rowardennan

Reaching the Loch, Mountain Issues
& The Canvas Bites Back

No thinking time required for this one, dear reader. Definitely a strawberry day, I mean just look at it. Dressed, packed and ready for action I make my way from the hotel. My oversized pack noisily and clumsily banging against the walls of the narrow hallways as I go. I continue on through the empty streets of Drymen, where I pick up the main road that will lead me back to the point of the trail where I veered off yesterday. It's not yet 7am and the dull grey of the morning light is darkened further by the ominous presence of immense storm clouds that loom moodily overhead. I leave the roadside to join a track that runs in a straight line towards a large area of forest that Mr B. advises me I will be remaining in for some time to come.

I'm once again amidst the dark and gloomy uniformity of manmade plantation woodlands. This is clearly a far older example than yesterday's however, which only serves to thicken and intensify the blackness, as the mature and imposing trees allow little or no sunlight to peek through their dense plumage. The moss-covered floor and frequent distant scurrying sounds of unidentified miniature furry feet strengthen the sense of impending danger. All nonsense of course, but the faithful old grey matter is once again helpless to prevent the aforementioned associations of atmospheric scenes such as this with monstrous creatures and gruesome, grizzly ends. Whilst - as previously discussed - I do enjoy the ambience unique to such a spooky locale (and taking into account that you already know me to be a heroic adventurer, unfazed by such childish fancies), I nevertheless decide it prudent to steer the creative little grey cells in another direction.

For the first time today, I mull over the Ben Nevis issue. It's the largest mountain in the UK and, when all is said and done, it's the climax of this hike. The issue though is whether or not it's possible for me to up the daily mileage to the required amount between now and the end of the trail. I'm intending to climb the smaller Ben Lomond later today, once I reach Rowardennan, meaning I'm already looking at upwards of 20-miles – so going any further than planned today is realistically out of the question. The stark truth therefore is that I'm already running out of days in which to find the extra 15-miles or so needed to pull it off. It's sobering stuff but at this juncture Ben Nevis is looking unlikely. I'd expect from your end, dear reader, the tension is really mounting here, eh? Will he, won't he? Can our hero rise to this, surely impossible, challenge against all the odds? Stay tuned.

I'm awakened from my daydreaming as the woods abruptly end and daylight washes over me. I walk into a wall of humid heat as I emerge from the cover of trees, although the day is still a grey one and the overhanging clouds that dominate the sky above me are beginning to work up a temper. I cross over a deserted road and straight into more woodland. The pines here are younger though, meaning I'm spared a return to thick monster-laden darkness for the time being. Just visible above the trees is the dashed pleasing sight of distant hilltops and mountain peaks and my pace quickens at the thought of what may lie beyond the forest. I pass through an area full of tents on either side of the path. All are silent save for one on my left, where a young chap sits cross legged by its entrance and patiently waits for the contents of a small saucepan to heat over a portable gas stove.

The path continues through the woods for what feels like an age. I'm not one to grumble, as you know. After all, the going is still easy and pleasant enough and I'm accompanied by a continued chorus of birdsong that would brighten the mood of even the most down-in-the-mouth of fellows. It's just that I've still got that lingering feeling that the thing hasn't really got going yet. Still on the runway so to speak. Eventually I reach a wide dirt track and turn left out of the woods to follow it for a short spell. The slightly dampened spirit is briefly encouraged to muster something approaching a small soar, as the best view of the day waves a hearty "Hello" up ahead. I get my first sight of Loch Lomond in the far distance. Again though, all the really good stuff still seems to be just out of reach and after a few minutes I'm plunged into woodland once more.

The path slowly ascends as it continues through the trees. After another mile or so I do finally reach the end of the forest. This time the spirit manages a full-blown soar to rival any, as I'm met by the welcome sight of a path winding off through dramatic open moorland. The striking Conic Hill is up ahead and Mr B. has already given me the heads up that I'll be climbing it shortly. The first decent ascent of the trail. The clouds pick this moment to unleash the first drops of rain, which seems in keeping with the rugged and windswept landscape stretching off in front of me. I stroll on with renewed purpose now, following the rocky undulating path through the bracken as it winds its way onward toward Conic Hill. A sparse peppering of hardy sheep wanders the desolate land around me, showing no reaction whatsoever to the increasing rainfall.

I cross a fast-flowing stream on a slippery footbridge that stands isolated on the otherwise featureless terrain. A short while later I reach the foot of the hill and begin my ascent. The rain stops just as suddenly as it had begun but is replaced by a bracing wind as the path rises up. The hill is 500 feet high but after the flat and easy walking of the last day and a half it may as well be Everest. I'm working up a sweat by the time I'm half way up and my pace is slowing. The trusty pack starts to weigh heavy and the old muscles even begin to ache – but I'm grinning like a hapless idiot as the track continues up the heather-covered hillside. This is the first instance on the trail where I've had the feeling of being a sole moving dot on a vast open landscape, and it instantly puts me on a giddy high. Eventually I reach the top, briefly leaving the trail to make the final rocky climb to the peak… And there it is.

It's as if the West Highland Way had risen from its slumber to stand tall before me. The delayed but grand entrance of the show's main star, accompanied by an unseen heavenly choir singing loudly in harmony: TAH-DAH! The deep rich blue of Loch Lomond sensationally sprawls itself across the view. A series of islands of varying sizes and shapes are exploding through the reflective surface of the water to emphasize the scale of the scene. Beyond that gigantic mountains with their peaks partially obscured by the low-hanging clouds. The Arrochar Alps and Ben Lomond are amongst them but I'm hanged if I can say which they are. I stand on the summit letting the wind rage through me – if the smile plastered on my face during the climb made me look like a hapless idiot then I must now have the crazed look of a chap filed firmly in the 'best avoided' category.

I sit myself down, deciding that only one thing can enrich this moment further; a Mars Bar. I unsheathe the first MB of the day and sit staring wide-eyed and transfixed at the stunning view. As I sit a smattering of fellow revellers begin to emerge. A few travelling in the same direction as myself along the trail, but most appearing over the crest of the hill in front of me. No doubt making the climb up from nearby Balmaha, where the trail will lead me shortly. The strength of the wind prevents any meaningful conversation but during the course of the next ten minutes or so I take part in an increasingly elaborate series of expressive facial exchanges, as we all seek to convey our appreciation of the vista. Reluctantly I tear myself away, conscious that I still have a lot of walking to do, and begin the descent towards the loch.

After only a minute or two the shelter of the peak behind me means the fierce wind instantly stops and a strange quiet calm engulfs me. I hear the murmur of conversation and then spy three figures on the path up ahead. As I home in on them it becomes apparent that one is a guide of some sort, talking enthusiastically to the other two. The guide is a shaven-headed chap adorned in fleece and a kilt (the first I've seen since crossing the border), and his enthralled audience are a middle-aged couple in brightly-clad and expensive looking walking gear, complete with poles and shiny mirrored sunglasses. He seems to be imparting a potted history of the area and, as casually as I can muster, I decide to mosey on over and have a listen.

I spend a short while listening to the fellow talk about fault lines and how we are standing on the exact boundary fault of the Highlands. I would go on, dear reader, but unfortunately it is at this point that my eyes glaze over and the theme tune to the classic 80's sci-fi series Quantum Leap starts playing in my head and drowning out the guide's words. I'm afraid this does happen from time to time. Often, it's whilst at work - but really it can be anytime when someone is explaining something to me that I'm failing to grasp. It doesn't have to be Quantum Leap you understand. In fact, only the other day Tasha was attempting to explain to me the finer aspects of the geology in and around our home city of Bristol. As soon as she said the word 'Ordovician' the eyes duly clouded over and the title music to A Question of Sport started loudly bouncing off the walls of the old cranial echo chamber. I'm unsure exactly how

31

much time passed but when the world came back into focus Tasha had stopped talking and was once again giving me 'that look.' It's a difficult look to describe... It's something akin to the look you might give to a cat that you've just run over with your car, as you stand staring down at it, deciding whether or not the kindest thing to do might be to just whack it over the head with a shovel. Not an angry look as such... more *concerned*.

With a few well-timed nods and concurring facial expressions I excuse myself and continue on my way. After some time making a steady descent down the open hillside I come to a waymarker advising me to take a left turning. The landscape becomes rocky here and I'm now descending at a much steeper rate. The path follows a thin ridge as it winds round to the right. The open grassland has been replaced by a thick covering of gorse, which perfectly suits the rough-and-tumble feel of this stretch. The grey skies of earlier have changed too. Although the dramatic clouds still linger above they have parted to reveal a backdrop of cornflower blue. The sun is also now blindingly visible and the further down the hillside that I get (away from winds) the hotter it becomes. This is fantastic walking and I feel a buzzing confidence that the trail has finally sparked into life. There are more people about now as well. My cautious downward progress on the tricky single-file track is being regularly halted to make way for panting passers-by, on their way up the steep hillside. The views are eventually broken as I reach a wooden gate that leads me into a wood of young spruce and pine trees.

This leads me in time to the edge of a large car park. I wander through, slightly dazed, as families unpack their picnics and lace up their hiking boots. Scores of cheerful mutts with tails wagging run around excitely in anticipation of imminent walkies. I spy a thistle-adorned waymarker and turn right onto a busy road leading to Balmaha Bay. I stroll along the edge of

Loch Lomond for the first time and soak up my charming surroundings. Sailboats and small passenger ferries rest on the still and tranquil water as it sparkles in the bright sunshine. On land the small tourist hotspot bustles with activity as countless thick-socked ramblers mingle amongst the families and coach parties of day-trippers. A melee of unfolding maps, selfie sticks and melting ice creams.

I stop for lunch by a handsome life-sized bronze statue of a hiker, resting against a stone wall. I'm mildly miffed to discover that Mr B. can tell me precisely nothing regards this moustachioed monument – but through the wonders of modern technology I can report that the good old phone steps up admirably. The detailed statue is in honour of one Tom Weir; an outdoorsman who hosted a popular TV show on Scottish television for many years and was something of a national treasure. I snap a few pics of the smiling chap and sit myself down to consume a couple of tasty processed stringy cheese things. It would be easy to forget the miles still ahead of me and remain in this sunny spot for the duration. Luckily yours truly is made of sterner stuff and after only a few minutes I'm hauling the pack on to the shoulders once more and gallantly setting off.

Afternoon

The road comes to a dead-end as I veer right up some steps for a short steep and muddy climb, only to then come straight back down again. After this bracing interlude the path settles into a very pleasant waterside jaunt that enables me to get better acquainted with the grand old loch. I wind my way through rich and varied woodland and past miniature cove-like clearings as the track clings to the water's edge. Sometime later I reach another car park and rejoin the road. Frustratingly I'm then drawn away from the water for a spell as I continue to follow the roadside before eventually heading back into woodland. These woods are a far cry from the straight-lined plantations of the previous two days however. My knowledge of trees is at a very similar level to my knowledge of geology – in that I have no knowledge of trees. That being said, I know a mighty old oak when I see one and there's a few of them standing proud along this stretch. Everything feels so densely packed here, in arresting contrast to the open moorland of a few hours ago. There's an almost jungle feel to my surroundings. Despite how well defined the route is I have a pleasing sensation of wandering at random through the undergrowth.

A few miles later I come across a large sign advising me that wild-camping is not permitted along this stretch of the loch. It takes a few minutes for this to sink in as I'm contentedly plodding along in my own world, but soon enough realisation dawns. As previously eluded to - tonight was set to be the first under the canvas and only the second-time wild camping in my brief but illustrious career as a fearless adventurer. That would be mistake number three of the trip, dear reader. Those keeping score will note I'm now averaging more than one major boob per day... At this rate I should be in hospital before the weekend.

Remarkably I have some signal on my phone and so at the next clearing I call round the nearby campsites. All are full. I try the YHA in Rowardennan to be told that this too is full for the night. Likewise, the Rowardennan Hotel. Just as my usually calm demeanour is beginning to crack the tip-top gent at the YHA calls me back to advise they do have a small campsite beside the hostel that has spaces available. I heave a sigh of relief and get going once more. This is the kind of nail-biting drama you can expect when travelling with me, dear reader. Seatbelts on.

The path delivers a few abrupt climbs as it continues its rocky way along the edge of the loch. I'm regularly passing fellow walkers as the afternoon beds in. In addition to people, I'm also sharing the trail with an increasing number of buzzing insects. This includes the occasional cloud of dreaded midges. Thus far I'm delighted to report that the advice of the aforementioned Ms A. Walker is proving sound enough and the Avon Skin So Soft is holding its own. I've been victim to the odd nibble of one kind or another but the dastardly midges seem to be keeping their distance and being suitably repelled. Whilst it's doubtless true that I stride through the dramatic highlands resembling a butter-basted oven-ready chicken, this seems a small price to pay to keep the relentless critters at bay.

The trail continues in this vein for a few more miles and the pack is again starting to weigh heavy when at last I emerge from the woodland, to once again re-join the road. I pass Rowardennan Hotel and am almost powerless to resist its outdoor beer garden overlooking the water. Yet I somehow drag my aching limbs past it to walk the last half a mile on to the YHA. After apparently annoying the gent at reception significantly by knocking on the kiosk window a full 10 minutes before official opening time, I'm begrudgingly given directions to the campsite. This proves to be a small strip of land on the very water's edge, capable of housing no more than a dozen tents. It's a pleasingly beautiful and at this point deserted spot. I set up the tent overlooking the water. I achieve this in only triple the time that the accompanying leaflet advises me it will take. I'm quite pleased with this.

I rest here for 30 minutes or so and contemplate heading off once more to climb the 974 metres of Ben Lomond. Once rested I leave all but the absolute essentials in the tent and haul my sorry carcass back along the path to the hotel, where the mountain trail begins. What a guy. There are a few different routes one can take up Ben Lomond... I plump for the easiest 'tourist route'. (Give me a break, I'm cream-crackered). There's a steady stream of people starting off at the same time as me and we all march in a line uphill through the woods. After a short while the path leaves the cover of trees to reveal the pending challenge in its entirety. A winding single-file track clings to the side of an impossibly steep hillside which rises up endlessly before me, to the extent that I'm unable to see the top. My muscles, quite reasonably under the circumstances, emit a small wince at the prospect.

On reflection I may have been too tired to make this journey after a decent length hike. As evidence of this I probably stand out rather amongst the steady line of climbers, being the only one not marvelling at the increasingly spectacular views during the ascent. My head is down and my hands are on my hips as though I'm permanently lunging forward as part of some relentless exercise routine. The Avon Skin So Soft has melted limply away and the sweat is soon pouring from me. By the time I reach something close to the halfway point I'm feeling as though I might not see the summit.

A group of teens who passed me early on at breakneck speed are now sitting looking decidedly grumpy and red-faced off to the side of the track. Indeed – looking around – the scene has something of the battlefield about it, with casualties strewn about the place in varying degrees of discomfort. I join them and plonk myself down on the ground for a few minutes. The views really are something special. The splendour of Loch Lomond with its mountainous backdrop is something I can't imagine ever tiring of. The spirit rallies and I pick myself up with renewed pluckiness. A woman, a few decades my senior, walks past as I'm doing this and gives me a hearty pat on the back. With this simple unspoken act of encouragement my tiredness seems to abate and I'm filled with a sense of comradeship towards my fellow climbers. I offer my hand to a nearby chap struggling to his feet and suddenly the world is a place full of smiling kindred spirits.

As I continue upwards I start to sing mountain-related songs to myself to keep the spirits up. I kick off with a rendition of *Move Any Mountain* by The Shamen then go straight into *Ain't No Mountain High Enough* (the Marvin Gaye and Tammi Terrell version – obviously). I soon realise that I don't know any other mountain-themed songs and so make some up by altering the words to other well-known hits. 'I'm a mountain man, hallelujah, I'm a mountain man ooohooh' (*It's Raining Men*), 'I can climb a mountain called Ben tonight, oh yeah' (*In the Air Tonight* – Phil Collins) and my personal favourite: 'You can tell many things by the way I walk, I've got cramps and sores, too tired to talk... Ben Lomond, Ben Lomond' (*Night Fever*).

Eventually – mercifully – the path levels out slightly and I can see the final destination up ahead. The summit of Ben Lomond is a jagged thin ridge that itself is almost as jaw-dropping as the views you get whilst standing on it. The wind is inevitably fierce but I'm immensely glad of it, as it cools me down instantly. As I stand atop the mountain peak looking out over a panoramic view that incorporates the whole of Loch Lomond, the Campsie Fells, the Arrochar Alps and so much more besides, I feel something of the magic of this place wash over me. Gazing out at adventures past and some of those yet to come over the next few days, I get goosebumps for the second time today. I zip up my coat as all about me do the same and after a short while turn and begin the long and slow descent back down to the loch.

I won't bore you with details of the descent, dear reader. For the most part it would just be me grumbling on about my aching feet... And nobody wants to hear any more of that. I will relay to you my surprise however, at the number of people I pass still making their way up as I descend. With afternoon giving way to the orange glow of evening I briefly wonder how late into the night the constant stream of climbers will continue to adorn this distinctive mountain. When I reach the bottom I rightly conclude that I don't have it in me to get back to the tent and so I head straight to the nearby hotel bar for dinner.

There is one vegetarian option on the menu: Pizza. I'll level with you: I'm more than a little fond of pizza. In fact, I could eat pizza everyday… Which is fortunate as that appears to be how things are shaping up. Not a turnip in sight on this occasion I'm somewhat relieved to confirm.

I spend a wholly enjoyable hour or two sat in the beer garden chomping down the aforementioned tomato and cheese flatbread concoction and slurping down a couple of rather robust ales for good measure. I then coax the old muscles into one last action for the day and make the short walk back to the campsite.

Not feeling quite ready to embrace the allure of the canvas just yet I decide that a night cap in the hostel is in order.

Rowardennan seems to only really consist of the hotel and the youth hostel. Both are picturesque, however. The hostel is a large old converted Victorian house complete with its own jetty.

After purchasing a bottle of ale, I make my way into the main living area (where one is encouraged to consume one's beverages). It has several impressive bay windows overlooking the loch. It is also choc-full of people. I choose a book from the collection laid out and find a good spot with a decent view in front of one of the windows.

I'm instantly struck by the number of different languages being spoken amongst the various groups gathered throughout the large room. Spanish, French and German are all definitely included, plus a few others I'm unsure of.

Everyone is young, too… which I suppose isn't hugely surprising given that I'm in a youth hostel. Nevertheless, it does get me thinking about the fact that many of the fellow walkers I've encountered so far have been of a younger age than I would perhaps have expected. Since discovering a passion for long distance hiking I've noted that, in terms of the general demographic, I'm something of a youngster. A dynamic young buck, so to speak. Indeed, I've oft congratulated myself on rooting out possibly the only hobby going at my age where this would still be the case.

Looking at this crowd, though, I'm something closer to an elder statesman.

I notice a couple of youngsters glancing in my direction whilst in conversation and imagine them to be saying something along the lines of:

'Hey, who's the cool-looking mature guy over there?'

'Isn't he that author who wrote that awesome book about walking the English coast?'

'Wow, I bet he's got some stories to tell. I hope I'm like him when I reach that age.'

Of course, I suppose it may just as easily have been:

'Hey, who's that creepy old guy sat in the corner drinking on his own?'

'Don't know... Don't look at him.'

I decide it's more likely the former and cheerfully open up my chosen book – a thriller called '*A Tap On the Window*' by Linwood Barclay – when a middle-aged couple walk into the room.

As if to provide final confirmation of the passing of my youth, they glance around the room and upon spotting me, head straight over. They're a friendly couple from somewhere in Kent, also walking the trail. We share a beer and chat about the walk so far, as well as what's still to come. The thing of most significance that results from this encounter is their total insistence that I must climb Ben Nevis.

'It would be like walking out of a film ten minutes from the end. It's the big finale of the whole hike.'

I boldly resolve to move heaven and earth in order to conquer the thing, there and then. For some reason, three ales into the evening it suddenly seems a good deal more achievable

I make my tipsy way to the tent just in time to watch the sun finally set on a long and memorable day.

It takes about half an hour of lying awake in the confined space for me to remember everything I dislike re the whole camping experience. I'm impossibly uncomfortable and see no realistic prospect of sleep ahead.

I employ the techniques I've picked up - as a one-time fully-fledged and paid up member of the insomniac community - to help see me through. Focus on your breathing, clear your head, all that stuff. A few hours pass in that strange state of mind between sleep and wakefulness. Then at some point in the early hours I finally drift off.

At 3am I'm woken by the strange sensation of having my feet gently pricked by a thousand small needles. In my semi-conscious state, I have a good old explorative rummage around down there. I soon discover that my feet and ankles are covered in tiny insects who are having a thoroughly enjoyable time biting every bit of exposed skin they can find. I expect it's as jolly and enjoyable a morning as any of the members of this particular community of creepy crawlies cares to remember.

After a small delay, wherein contemplation of my predicament fully dawns, I leap into action. I clamber from the tent, where I then decide to do a small war dance for a few moments. After which I scratch crazily at my feet and ankles, brushing off all the remaining diners as I do so. I try, completely in vain, to clear the rest of the little blighters from the tent- giving the sleeping bag a ruddy good shake down in the process.

Then I buckle down to the main scratching session. After an unspecified period of time has elapsed - once my feet and ankles are red raw and hundreds of small red lumps have started to appear all over them – I climb back into the tent. I don't cry... I'd like to make that clear at this point. Many an adventurer would do so I know, but not I. I'd expect Ray Mears would be sobbing for his mother by now. I merely sit, huddled in one corner of the infested shelter, defeated once again by the camping experience, and wait for sunrise.

DAY THREE

Crianlarich

Rowardennan

Day 3: Rowardennan to Crianlarich

Itchy Feet, Rocky Climbs & Liquid Bubblegum.

This really is beyond the pale. I've never actually understood exactly what 'the pale' is per se – but if I've correctly grasped the general gist of the idiom then I can confirm that I am currently well beyond it. *Well beyond it*, dear reader. So far beyond the foresaid pale am I that if I were to turn back and look behind me the pale would barely be visible, little more than a distant speck. The pale and I are no longer acquainted. And good riddance. I shall not mourn the passing of the pale. The pale, as far as I'm concerned, can go hang. I'm shoving the canvas and all of its cursed appendages back into their maddeningly miniscule bag. The sun has yet to make any meaningful appearance but there is just enough light for me to see that the inside of the tent still crawls with hordes of tiny scurrying assassins. I've no idea what they are (my insect knowledge being at a similar level to my knowledge of trees and geology) and frankly I don't need to know at this juncture. I just want this confounded tent out of my sight. When it's finally scrunched into the bag I head off, still under the cover of relative darkness.

I'm sorry to report that, as you may well have gathered, the spirits are somewhat deflated. My feet and ankles are on fire, I'm tired and becoming decidedly irritable. The first thing I do as I slump back to join the path is turn on the phone and log on to Booking.com. I book a room at the only available lodgings within a day's walk from here. A wooden cabin in a village called Crianlarich, over 23-miles away. A long walk but, as I need to make up time re Ben Nevis and as it's not yet 5am, I figure it's doable. The thought of a real bed at the end of the day temporarily lifts the cloud of gloom encircling me. I glance down and notice that my trousers are on back-to-front.

As I continue along the broad dirt track my mood darkens yet further. Am I doomed to be the laughing stock of the hiking community? A fearless explorer that can't stomach camping. Indiana Jones with his trousers on the wrong way around. How many miles can one man carry a tent without actually using it? Would Bear Grylls have booked into a bed-and-breakfast at the first whiff of infestation? No, he wouldn't. He'd have gathered up the little critters and eaten them for breakfast. They'd have rued the day. He probably wouldn't even have seasoned them… just crunched them up and washed them down with a bottle of his own urine. Speaking of breakfast… I reach into my pack for a trusty Weetabix drink. I pull out a banana flavoured bottle and decide to go with it, let fate decide. Be more adventurous. It turns out that after a few days of being carried around in a backpack under the sweltering July sun a Weetabix drink is liable to start curdling. I swig it down anyway, I'd like to think that's what Bear would have done.

I consult Mr B. regards the day ahead, to be advised that today's stretch is the toughest of the entire trail. As I read the words 'fearsome reputation' in reference to what awaits me I'm finally able to regain some focus. I apply the stiff upper lip and cast aside my self-pity to face the challenge before me with renewed vigour. It simply won't do to mope about feeling sorry for myself when there's good hiking to be had. I'm in one of the most staggeringly beautiful landscapes in the world and I'm damned if I'm going to let an aversion to camping ruin it for me. Besides, it isn't as though I need to tell anyone is it? I mean as far as anyone knows I did eat the little critters for breakfast. Come to think of it, dear reader, drinking your own urine and eating tree bark and such like is all good and well, but could Bear Grylls survive on a diet consisting exclusively of processed stringy cheese snacks and Mars Bars? I mean I doubt it, dear reader, I really do.

The path is gently ambling through woodland adorned with more fine examples of the noble oak, and daylight is at last beginning to creep through the leaves and illuminate my surroundings. After a few minutes, once the misery of the previous few hours has been replaced by a chipper enthusiasm for the journey ahead, the track takes me back down to the edge of the loch. Oak trees continue to tower above the path, but all below them is dramatically changed. The wide dirt track is replaced by a thin strip winding its way off through the undergrowth. It clings to the water's edge as it goes around, over and even under rocks and boulders along the way. Despite the dry early morning heat the going is muddy and increasingly slippery. Exposed tree roots are proving a particularly greasy hazard. There is again that feeling of exploring off the beaten track, as the path itself is often partially obscured in the dense tangle of jungle landscape.

The going is progressively strenuous as well. I'm constantly negotiating steep slippery ascents and descents. The climbs are always short, but what they lack in scale they make up for in frequency. The cobwebs are being well and truly brushed away and - although the pack seems even larger and clumsier than normal in these enclosed conditions - I'm moving at a decent pace. After a mile or two Mr B. tells me to keep an eye out for Rob Roy's prison. A cave amongst the rocks where, rumour has it, the outlaw turned folk hero used to imprison his unfortunate hostages. This turns out to be easy enough to spot, in no small part due to the large white letters spelling out the word CAVE that a helpful passer-by has written in chalk at the entrance. I briefly entertain the idea of investigating further and clambering into the rocky darkness. I'm on something of a roll however and am enjoying the scrambling trek, so I decide to march on.

The walking continues in this challenging manner for another couple of miles. All the while the still water of Loch Lomond sparkles serenely by my side. By the time the path rises steeply up into an area of woodland, I've sweated off the old Avon SSS and need to pause to catch my breath. I now find myself in a moss-covered conifer wood. The bright greens of the mossy carpet against the darker shade of the Christmassy conifers gives the scene a pleasing enchanted forest feel. It's almost cartoon-like and I can imagine the Gummi Bears, Bert Racoon or any number of other animated characters from my childhood appearing from the darkness. Perhaps this is an early warning sign that the lack of sleep is catching up with me. In any event, the walk through the magical cartoon forest is a pleasant one. As I stroll onwards my stream of consciousness takes me on a whistlestop tour through the television shows of my youth. I'm whistling the theme tune to Count Duckula by the time I spy the first bothy of my Highland adventure coming into view up ahead.

I've never encountered a bothy before and as such I'm excited by the prospect. These basic stone structures (in effect the shell of an old disused house or cottage) are left unlocked and free for anyone to use. Rowchoish bothy is a fine example (well… I mean to say, I assume so… As I've just admitted I've never actually seen one before. Technically it could be the worst bothy in the entire world I suppose, how would I know?) that looks as though it may have started life as a barn or stables. I indulge in a tentative nose around only to find it deserted. It consists of one large stone room with an impressive open fireplace at one end. A few tables and chairs dotted about the place suggest that it is looked after in some capacity, perhaps by a local volunteer group. They also give the place an eerie, ghostly atmosphere and I suddenly feel as though I'm trespassing in a house from a forgotten time. Only yesterday I may have been cheerily considering the bothy as a potential alternative to pitching the tent. Today however my bruised ego, along with the rest of my sorry personage, needs a long hot soak in a (preferably private) bathtub and some fluffy clean pillows for good measure. On cue I notice that I'm absentmindedly scratching away once more at my bloody and inflamed ankles. I take this as a hint that it's time to get going again and follow the path away from the bothy and back into the trees.

A brief respite follows as the track widens and flattens. This turns out to be nothing but a cruel trick however and within a few minutes I've resumed my uncoordinated scramble, as I'm lead back down to the water's edge. Over the next mile or so the path criss-crosses through a number of arrestingly beautiful mini-waterfalls. These provide even greater richness to the sense of tropical wilderness that has characterised the day's walk so far. I arrive at a footbridge that takes me over the flowing water of Cailness Burn. It also gives me some spectacular views of the loch. The panoramas I'm being regularly treated to seem to be becoming ever more dramatic; the jagged peaks of Glen Falloch that populate the skyline here are no exception. The going then starts to get even trickier. A difficult, steep rocky climb is immediately followed by a perilous descent. It's worth noting at this point, dear reader, that as far as this section of the trail goes - when I report a rocky climb, I mean it literally. It's not just a slightly exaggerated way of saying I walked up a steep hill (as it *may* or may not have been every other time I've made such a claim). I am actually climbing over rocks. I'm using my hands and everything. Take that, Grylls.

That being said, as I teeter along a thin ledge with a sheer drop to the water beside me, I do have to seek verification from Mr B. that I haven't wandered off course. Thankfully he confirms I'm still on track as well as taking the opportunity to point out that this stretch is a great place to catch site of mountain goats and deer. No luck in that regard I'm sad to report, although I'm not entirely alone. The dreaded midges are out in force along the edge of the loch. I'm intermittently passing through clouds of the little blighters and am receiving a good deal of unwanted attention. Nothing when compared with the angry alien land-masses that once called themselves my ankles of course, but I'm nevertheless definitely picking up more than the odd nibble. Just as I'm starting to doubt the advice of a certain A. Walker I recall that this morning's layer of the old Avon SSS has long since been sweated off. I stop to apply a fresh coating and as I do so glance down at my shiny arms and hands. If nothing else I will certainly end this trail with something of a silky radiant glow.

After a few more miles I arrive at another footbridge. This one will lead me over the largest and most impressive waterfall of the trail so far and on to the Inversnaid Hotel beyond. I stop for a moment halfway across the bridge and watch the impressive tide of water endlessly crashing down over the rocks with ferocious force. Once across I clamber down some steep steps that lead me round to the front of the large and imposing white Victorian building. It takes a good deal of self-discipline to walk past the somewhat grand hotel entrance without marching in, booking a room and running a steaming hot bubble bath. We Reynolds are made of sterner stuff however and, after negotiating a slightly confusing car park area, I pick up the trail again as it leaves the hotel behind.

I enjoy a short spell along a wide and easy-going track, adorned on either side with scores of colourful tents. The campers I pass contemplating their breakfasts are (I note for a second time) all relative youngsters and are speaking a variety of European languages. Their shrewd decision to set up camp within a stone's throw of a hotel complete with enticing bar facilities no doubt accounts for some of the bleary-eyed grimaces on display, as they emerge from the canvas into the bright morning sunshine.

Soon enough however I find myself again clambering over rocks, sliding down muddy hillsides and perspiring my way up endless crags. Whilst I'm now well on my way to physical tiredness the spirit remains wholeheartedly exhilarated by my rough-and-tumble surroundings. To my surprise I pass a second of Rob Roy's caves a short while later. I'd assumed the previous to be unique and the presence of this second hidey-hole diminishes my hither-to wide-eyed awe just a smidge. A sentiment strengthened when, upon observing the foresaid back-up, it appears to me to be little more than a stony crevice. I check-in with Mr B. who describes it in his own inimitable style as a 'gloomy cleft'... I find this description a good deal more amusing than I've any right to and am chuckling audibly to myself as I continue on my way.

As I begin to fall into something like a rhythm despite the continued tricky going, I even find time to gaze out across the loch at the tiny tree-covered island of Vow. Just as I'm noting that everything is looking a little bit Jurassic Park - and begin to daydream about T-Rexes emerging above the island's treeline – I happen upon a ladder. It's fixed to a sheer rockface blocking the path. After a few seconds confusedly staring at the thing the grey cells finally accept its presence to be fact and I begin to contemplate lugging the cursed pack up the wooden structure and over the rock-face to the continuation of the path above. It's as if the trail itself had clocked that I might be getting used to the tough walking and becoming a touch nonchalant and so conjured up a ladder in anger. My ascent is not an entirely dignified affair, but I am feeling a bit more like the pre-infestation fearless explorer of old, as I march onwards in the mid-morning heat. Despite the many steep climbs up hills and mountains since discovering a passion for hiking, this is definitely the first ladder I've encountered!

As I continue onwards I'm now regularly passing other walkers. One chap with a disgruntled teenager in tow stops me and asks me about my journey. He has walked the WHW in full on three separate occasions but is currently here on holiday with his family. We chat for a few minutes as his son stands in the background looking thoroughly bored and unmoved by his surroundings, with hands in pockets and eyes on the ground. He recommends a pub in Fort William at the end of the trail and we say our goodbyes. A few minutes later, at the top of a particularly unsporting hill I'm greeted by the smiling faces of two girls swigging from their water bottles.

'Nice day for a gentle stroll,' one of them remarks with a thick American accent. I'm certainly starting to sense the comradely spirit that this walk is known for. The wide-ranging demographic of folk I've encountered thus far have all had one thing in common. They've all been smiling.

Eventually the landscape around me begins to slowly change and I become aware that I'm approaching the end of the loch. The dense tree cover falls away but a couple of miniature beachfronts allow me a few more moments of contemplation, staring out across the motionless and beautiful water. The midges are present but keeping their distance (A. Walker is redeemed) and I'm lucky enough to spy a buzzard above the trees on the other side of the loch. As it circles and glides across the wondrous view I'm suddenly fearful of not spending enough time breathing in this place. The opaline (growth *and* maturity) water of Loch Lomond has been an ever-present over the last day and a half and as I head off into the unknown I feel a pang of pre-emptive nostalgia at leaving it behind.

The end of the loch itself is populated by a row of houses and a hotel. As I emerge from the jungle and into open farmland I consider for a moment what it must be like to call this place home. I pass a fenced off old bothy that stands abandoned, slowly crumbling out of existence – its inhabitants and their own stories of life on the loch all long forgotten. The going underfoot is now decidedly easier and I'm walking along a cobbled track as sheep and Highland cattle graze in the fields to my right. The water itself is populated too; passenger ferries pass by each other as holidaymakers wave cheerily and scores of ducks and guillemots float dozily by. I reach a footbridge as the path begins to curve and for the first time all week I'm now walking away from the water.

A steep climb follows soon after and affords me a further opportunity for reflection. The path travelled and the journey ahead both greet me at the summit. Behind me one last majestic view of Loch Lomond and in front of me an open wilderness of mountain peaks. It's a goosebumps moment that sweeps away my tiredness and any sense of sadness at leaving the loch behind. All the adventures yet to come are calling to me now and telling me to pull my finger out and stop already with all this reflection and contemplation malarkey. Just get a jog on, will you? And bring your boots, you're gonna need them. There's a spring back in the old step as I head off towards the village of Inverarnan, where I'll stop for lunch.

Inverarnan turns out to be a touch further down the good old road than I'd previously assumed it to be. Luckily my new-found forward-thinking attitude just about sustains me through the extra miles. I cross endless fields and marshland and it feels exhilarating to be out in the open space again. Another climb yields more breath-taking views – this time of the River Falloch that snakes its way off into the distance ahead of me. Eventually the path heads downwards at a steep angle until it emerges, via a stretch of woodland, into a flat area of lush-green pasture. I come across a sign pointing in the direction of Inverarnan – but I never get all the way into the village. A huge campsite advertising food & drink for sale distracts me en route and I decide that this will be the spot for an overdue lunch.

The campsite is vast, with wooden lodges, caravans and tent pitches as far as the eye can see. I head for the outdoor seating area next to the café and, having shed The Albatross from my back, collapse onto a bench. I wolf down a few sweaty and bendy stringy cheese snacks and the daily Mars Bar before taking a gulp of unpleasantly warm water. I'm not feeling entirely refreshed and ready for action to be honest with you, dear reader. The old MB hits the spot as usual of course, but that apart, I'm slightly underwhelmed by the whole luncheon experience today. I decide to hobble into the café to see what's on offer. My eye is drawn to an open-front fridge in one corner filled exclusively with shiny orange cans of drink. The fabled Irn-Bru. I purchase said fizzy beverage and pay the somewhat grumpy looking fellow standing sullenly behind the counter. He remarks almost accusingly on how tired I look and scoffs - a touch unhelpfully I thought - when I tell him I'm only halfway through the day's walk.

'You certainly don't look ready for the second half,'

he says, with not even a hint of the jolly countenance I've so recently been proclaiming the whole of Scotland to possess. He stares at me briefly, awaiting my riposte. He receives none and instead I turn my back on the dour chap thinking to myself, 'Moody git, if my mum were here she'd sort you out and no mistake.' Ordinarily a kind and gentle soul; mother dearest will instantly transform into a bloodthirsty lioness at the merest whiff of threat to either of her – charmingly defective – cubs. She'd have sorted out those bally insects this morning that's for sure. They'd have been begging for some time alone with a hungry Bear Grylls long before mother dearest was through with them. Not that I'm under any threat from old Meldrew back there of course. In truth he's just some poor fellow stuck inside a hot café all day as endless streams of nauseatingly cheerful hikers roll in and attempt to engage him in inane conversation.

On my way back to the bench I open up the can and take a swig. My walk is halted mid-step. I stand nonplussed for a few seconds as my senses determine how best to process this new sensation. It's like refreshing liquid bubblegum coursing its way aggressively through my innards. Eventually my brain and body decide in unison that this is a pleasurable experience. I sit down and drink the rest of the can. Each mouthful is an event in itself. I smile and shake my head in a way that no doubt ensures my fellow diners will be careful to give me a wide berth for the remainder of my time here. At some point during the consumption of the remaining liquid I decide that I will only be drinking Irn-Bru from this moment on and for the rest of my days. Water now seems to have no meaning or purpose, likewise fruit juice or cola. Then I remember my Weetabix drinks and come abruptly to my senses. Then there's ale and whisky of course. No, on second thoughts… There is room in a chap's life for all these liquids… No need to be hasty in matters such as this. Nevertheless, this feels like a watershed moment in my Scottish adventure. Now I just need to find someone who'll sell me a neep and/or a tattie. Suitably refreshed and positively raring to go, I sling the pack on the shoulders and march on like a thing possessed.

Afternoon

Mr B. advises that the afternoon's haul to Crianlarich will be a good deal easier going than this morning's stretch. Despite being rejuvenated by the 27-million tonnes of sugar contained within the nation's favourite fizzy drink, my achy muscles and still screaming itchy ankles are immeasurably pleased to hear this news. Indeed, I'm currently sauntering contentedly along a wide and flat dirt track. The River Falloch is now alongside me and beyond it the never welcome sight of a main road. Somewhere further still in that direction there is a railway line, but I'm seeing no evidence of it as yet. Despite the road the scenery is nonetheless attractive. The river flows fast and frantically amidst jagged rocks and on the other side of the track I'm passing through vibrant patches of dense woodland. I'm also continuing to pass other walkers as I go, and at one-point exchange hellos with a lady that bears more than a passing resemblance to my dear grandmother.

If you're reading there is, in my estimation, a one in ten chance you received your copy of the book from my grandmother. (Hi, Grandma.) Certainly, that will be the case if the previous book is anything to go by. For a few days there the good folks over at Amazon may have thought they had an international bestseller on their hands as my grandma purchased copies for everyone she knows, and a few spares for anyone she may meet in passing. The only successful book signing of my literary career thus far was conducted at her kitchen table as I wrote personalised messages in piles of books for her friends around world and numerous family members (including a few I'm not entirely sure that I knew even existed). On another occasion she insisted that my grandad drive her down to the hotel at Hartland Quay (a place I mention in the book), with a copy in tow, and essentially force them to add it to their selection of books available for guests to read. My grandad duly obliged - though quite reasonably would rather, when all is said and done, have been getting a few hours in down at the bowls club with the chaps. He doubtless knew better than to voice this opinion however, and who can blame him?

For you see, we Reynolds menfolk have a long-running tendency to pair off with women at the more dominant, 'relationship trouser-wearing' end of the spectrum.

(Stepmother Jane and my own dearest Natasha will no doubt add credence to this claim.) Actually - it may not be gender specific as such – I'll need to check this with my brother Mark and his partner Tom. Although now that I think of it I do have it straight from the horse's mouth that the heating in their house only goes on when Tom is good and ready for it to do so (which, as I understand it, is usually for approximately three hours during the last week of January). So perhaps it's safe to assume that the Reynolds contingent isn't the primary trouser wearer in that particular household either. Not that we can't put our respective feet down on any given subject from time to time of course. Au contraire; we Reynolds can put foot to floor with the best of them. We just tend to wait until the object of our affections is well out of earshot before doing so. Better safe than sorry and all that. Anyway, I digress; the point being – when I do eventually achieve national treasure status and become the world's premier travel writer – it will doubtless be because my grandma has mastered the internet and launched a global marketing campaign based on intimidation and the hard-sell. Which is fine by me.

My daydreaming is interrupted by the sight of more spectacular waterfalls. This section of the trail is full of them and long may it continue. I stand and stare as the roaring waters crash against the rocks and drown out the hum of traffic from the road behind me. The path begins to undulate now and I'm alternating between wood-covered valleys and far-reaching views. Another of the mighty Highland mountains comes into view in the background and it suddenly seems as though this once slow-to-get-going trail, is now showing off: mountains, waterfalls, mountains, waterfalls. It's certainly strange to think that only 48 hours ago I was voicing concern at the lack of Highland splendour this trail was delivering. I'm learning fast that a single day of the West Highland Way is capable of transporting you through contrasting landscapes at a rate that most other trails can only hope to manage in a week.

As if in a nod of agreement, the surroundings begin to change again. The path flattens out and both the river and the road beyond it get a good deal closer. The weather is changing as well; the heat is still of brow-wiping intensity but the fierce yellow sun has been obscured from view by vast angry swirling clouds of black and grey, that engulf the far-away mountain peaks once more. A footbridge guides me across a babbling stream and I'm then climbing once again. As I reach the crest of the hill the path joins an old disused military road. This helps to make the view ahead all the more beautiful. The rocky old dirt road winds off through the rugged windswept landscape. A drystone wall runs down one side, separating me from fields sparsely populated with hardy sheep and Highland cattle. The accompanying farmhouse and outbuildings are just visible in the distance.

Closer to hand though is the slightly surreal sight of a single deck chair stood to the side of the path. A large cold-box is perched on top of it and a small honesty box underneath. I open it up to discover it's full of cold cans of Irn-Bru and Mars Bars. All it's missing is a sign saying 'Here you go, Steve.' I briefly wonder if this is an hallucination – am I actually here, or in fact unconscious in a hospital bed after being found covered in poisonous insect bites in a smelly tent in Rowardennan? I duly dispense a couple of quid in the honesty box and enjoy an unscheduled afternoon snack. Not for the first time I consider the possibility of there being a dose of hearty Scottish blood somewhere in the old S. Reynolds heritage. I mean to say any nation of peoples that scatters boxes of Mars Bars about the countryside for the weary traveller to enjoy must surely be cut from the same cloth as yours truly?

I crack on with the wide-eyed intensity peculiar to a fellow happily overdosing on refined sugar. The railway line that has been covertly running alongside the river and road for the last few miles now becomes visible. Path, river, road and railway line all now carve their way through the arresting and unforgiving terrain in resolute unison. I cross the river at one point and again allow myself a moment to watch the flowing water run ceaselessly by on its never-ending journey. The path splits from the old military road but continues in very much the same vein. More waterfalls follow shortly after as do more brief strolls amongst the birch woods. I'm enjoying having the path to myself for a spell, with nobody in view in either direction. I branch out into song, inspired by a combination of my wondrous surroundings and additional sugar intake. The Scottish Highlands is treated to an off-key rendition of Carter USM's (the greatest band in musical history – fact) genre-defining classic *The Only Living Boy in New Cross*. As is the way of these things when I'm alone in the wilderness my brain gets stuck on the chorus line *'The good, the bad, the average and unique'* and I end up subconsciously chanting 'average and unique, average and unique' over and over as I walk on. Some people come out into the wilderness and compose poetry, other's use the peace and tranquillity to thrash out all of their day-to-day problems. I on the other hand tend to walk hundreds of miles repeating single lines of songs or meaningless mantras – like a broken robot.

My latest earworm is mercifully interrupted as the path dips down to cross underneath the railway line. The dirt track gives way to a small tunnel lined with what looks like corrugated iron. Fearing I've taken a wrong turning I consult Mr B., who advises me that this is a sheep creep and confirms that I do indeed need to walk through it. I bend down and shuffle onwards but the old Albatross kicks up a fuss and collides with the entrance roof. I take the great lump off the shoulders and drag it unceremoniously through the tunnel. Once through I notice the bag is now smeared - quite thoroughly - with sheep poo. 'Sorry, old thing,' I say – hopefully not out loud but I can't be sure. 'Ladders and sheep creeps, eh? We weren't really prepared for all this, old chum, were we?' I catch myself chatting away to an inanimate canvas bag in the nick of time as just then a group of fellow walkers appear, travelling in the opposite direction to myself. We briefly exchange pleasantries before they make their way through the tunnel with dexterity and ease (despite carrying equally large backpacks) and I plod on... Smelling of sheep poo.

That's the thing about The Albatross as far as this particular trip goes, dear reader. I can't even really have a moan about it. Everyone on this trail seems to have an Albatross of their own... Truth be told, mine's only mid-ranking in the old bag-to-person-ratio size stakes. When I walked the Coast Path last year I was constantly being told I'd overpacked. Complete strangers would make it their business to inform me of this fact. At first this was a touch demotivating and added to the whole 'I have no idea what I'm doing' look, which I was sporting at the time. By the end however, I'd managed to convince myself that carrying the thing had somehow added to my achievement. The West Highland Way has robbed me of this illusion. It's true that I've not packed quite as much useless stuff this time around, of course. (Growth and maturity.) It turns out that eight complete sets of clothes is excessive. Plus, emergency canned food is only effective if you have both a tin opener and a means of cooking said food. If you have neither then... Well you may as well have taken along a few house bricks for all the good they'll do you. The reason I'm struggling is, of course, my decision not to acclimatise to the extra weight by carrying the thing on a few hikes in the run up to the trail. For this reason, I shall endeavour not to bore you with any further whinge sessions regards any chafing or spine realignment, etc. And although I've settled on the 'Albatross moniker' – I hope the touching scene under the sheep creep adequately conveys my affection for the great old lump.

Things then get a bit confusing for a brief spell as I cross over a stream and then zig-zag across a patch of tarmac road. Just as I'm becoming disorientated I pass through a second tunnel, this time thankfully designed with humans in mind, to cross underneath the main road. A short uphill clamber ensues thereafter and leads me up to the very welcome sight of another disused military dirt road – winding its way back out into the open wilderness. In fact, it may well be the very same old military road as previously. The clouds are starting to part overhead and the striking patches of brilliant blue are increasing in size. Vast hills and mountains again frame the view up ahead and thick areas of conifer plantations pepper the unspoilt landscape. A chain of telephone wires dangle precariously across the scene as smatterings of unconcerned sheep graze idly below them. One of them looks up at me as I walk past, its jaw rhythmically churning a mouthful of murky green grass all the while. In a gesture that confirms I'm now entering the realms of sleep deprivation and total exhaustion I find myself waving to it cheerily. I could almost swear to you that it rolls its eyes at me before looking away and continuing to graze.

Despite the tiredness I feel I could walk this landscape for forever and a day. The going is now easy and the surroundings are soul-enrichingly grandiose. It's in an almost dream-like trance that I continue on my way in the intensifying afternoon heat. After a while I pass another farmstead sitting isolated and open to the elements. For the third time on this trip I find myself considering how incredible it must be to live out here. A world away from the headless chaos and neon-glow of city life. No traffic jams, no retail outlets, no cheap seats or executive boxes. It's very easy to idealise of course. Life out here is no doubt harsh and unforgiving in ways my pampered mind is unable to comprehend. The escape and adventure of the long-distance trail is not the same thing as calling a place home. Yet - for me - the path *itself* is home. I have felt this for a long time now. I'm only truly at peace when following a trail to wherever it may lead me. In that sense my desires are as far-removed from the pressures and routines endured by the occupants of this picturesque farm as they are from the crowded streets and concrete office buildings of the city. A gypsy heart perhaps – as long as I don't have to sleep in a tent and can end the day with a bubble bath and a single malt on the rocks. Sigh.

Although the going remains flat and thus relatively untaxing, the track itself is becoming less defined. The dry dirt and loose stone are being replaced by soggy mud and deceptively deep puddles. The old boots are taking something of a pounding as the day's long walk begins to slowly draw to a close. As the curve of the land changes a vast area of woodland looms into view. For a while it seems to remain eternally fixed on the horizon and never actually get any closer. I do eventually reach the edge of the wood however and (after squeezing the pack through a kissing gate) I reach for Mr B. to consult the map. I must leave the trail here and pick up another footpath that will lead me through the woods to Crianlarich.

I notice a couple of chaps up ahead at a crossroads where three tracks meet. One is sitting on a bench and the other is standing looking over him and giving off an air of impatience. The seated figure appears to have covered his entire body in clothing. His hood is pulled up and his face is covered by something resembling a scarf. His head is in his hands, which are gloved. It's a strange sight under the continued heat of the sun. As I pass by the standing figure looks at me and says:

'Midges… He's been eaten alive.'

'Oh no. Do you want some midge repellent?' I reply, foreseeing the need to explain why I'm using a beauty product to keep the midges at bay.

'No, you're alright thanks, mate. He's had some of mine now... He's overreacting.'

'F*** off,' comes the muffled retort from beneath the layers.

Feeling a strong pang of sympathy for the fellow I locate the path branching off to the right and get going again. The encounter seems to have reminded my ankles that they too have been eaten alive and they instantly resume screaming at me to scratch them until I hit bone. The path maintains a steady downhill gradient as it weaves through more of the pleasant plantation woodland that has defined huge chunks of this trail so far. It's cool under the cover of the trees and after ten minutes or so I even briefly entertain the idea of putting my coat on. I dismiss this idea however when I consider what it would involve. Stopping – taking off the pack, rooting around for the coat, etc. All out of the question re my current level of tiredness. As is so often the way at the end of a long hike. As soon as the end is nearly in sight every muscle waves the white flag and the last mile or so is suddenly all but an impossibility of effort. After a further ten minutes of continued downhill crawl I feel a second pang of sympathy. This time for the S. Reynolds of tomorrow morning, who will begin his hike with a relentless slog back up this hill.

I finally reach the end of the woodland and am greeted by the joyous sight of Crianlarich up ahead. I pretty much slide down the final descent to reach the side of the main road that has followed me all afternoon. After crossing it I then pass through the village's prominent railway station connected to the railway line that has also followed me all the way from Inverarnan. With map in tow I negotiate my way through the village to locate my bed for the night. Crianlarich is a pretty and characterful spot, seemingly built around the train station. A few thin streets with tightly packed cottages and houses make up the centre. I pass a striking war memorial and distinctive white church on my way through. I then join a second main road leading away from the village. Here the houses and buildings are much more sparsely populated and the character quickly changes to one of roadside cafés and B&Bs. The whole place seems to be completely deserted, save for the odd passing car. The walk along the pavement to my lodgings is probably only a few hundred yards but in my ungainly and aching state it seems to take an age. At last I see the complex of wooden lodges sitting beside a wondrously enticing pub, that will provide me with the rest and sustenance I require.

The girl that shows me to my cabin is friendly and welcoming with a rich and deep Scottish drawl.

'How far today then?' she says, clocking my exhaustion.

'About 23-miles,' I reply in a suitably sleepy tone.

'Ha, just away for a wee dauner then!'

I stare vacantly for a second or two.

'Eh?'

'A walk. Just a wee walk then?'

'Oh right, I see… What did you say? A doner… Like a kebab?'

'No, a dauner: D-A-U-N-E-R. Means walk… Do you know you've got your trousers on back-to-front?'

So then, dear reader, 'Just away for a wee dauner' would basically be Scottish for 'Just off for a walk'. I should probably write that down before I forget.

The cabin is basic but comfortable. Alas no bubble bath option, so I jump straight into the shower before collapsing onto the bed for a snooze. I awake with a start about an hour or so later and briefly wonder where on earth I am. The room is a wood-panelled square with two single beds, a table and chair and a separate shower cubicle and lavatory. I take a good look around and decide that (ignoring the television, fluffy towels, coffee making facilities and electric heaters) this is still *kind of* like camping. I mean I'm still within the adventurer ballpark here, surely? All things considered, it's a log cabin in the Scottish Highlands, right? I ponder this as I stand in front of the mirror applying first some moisturiser and then a dash of caramel flavoured lip balm. Then I put on some fresh clothes and head to the pub for a hearty cooked meal. Take that, Grylls.

The pub is a cosy and traditional tartan-carpeted number with white stone walls and a fireplace at one end. It's already busy, in direct contrast to the deserted world outside its four walls. I find a small round table towards the back of the room and peruse the menu. The only veggie option is macaroni cheese with garlic bread – which sounds grand to me and will make a novel change from pizza. The grub is decent and piled generously onto the plate. Whilst I'm munching contentedly the pub continues to fill up and I tune in and out of people's conversations regards the day's walking. Everyone here is a fellow hiker as far as I can fathom. A middle-aged German (I think) couple a few tables down from me chat with a waitress for a while and relay with infectious enthusiasm their adventure thus far.

This gets me thinking about my own experiences up to this point. If you discount Ben Nevis I've now reached the halfway point of the trail. What a few days it's been – and, if Mr B. is to be believed, the best is arguably yet to come. This is a heartening thought and I let it sink in for a few minutes as the trusty old digestive system sets about the considerable challenge of processing the mac 'n' cheese. I carry out a bit of a mental stocktake. Still zero sightings of the elusive golden eagle. One can but hope that situation rectifies itself. The heart is set. On the plus side however, I am on target regards the totter up Ben Nevis. One more plus-twenty-miler and a couple of decent fifteens will see me home, I fancy.

I bloatedly wander over to the bar and study the admirable selection of single malts lined up on display. The girl who showed me to my cabin earlier is now dressed in chef's whites and chatting to the bartender.

'You look a bit better, how was the kebab?' she says with a smile. I smile back apologetically and the confused looking bartender strolls over and asks me what I fancy to drink.

After some deliberation, during which any pretence that I may know anything even approaching what I'm talking about is categorically done away with, I plump for a peaty little offering from the good folk over at the Jura distillery. It goes down remarkably easily and a couple more follow hot on its heels. At some point during the second tipple I get chatting to the bartender for a few minutes and he enquires about my journey.

'Are you doing Ben Nevis?'

'Of course, it's the grand finale of the entire walk,' I reply, as if these words were my own and not those spoken to me by the couple I met in the youth hostel only last night. I go further still: 'Walking the West Highland Way and not doing Ben Nevis would be like walking out of the cinema ten minutes before the end of the movie. It's the climax, you know?' I can tell he's impressed by this.

'You're not wrong there, my friend. I've done it a few times myself. You'd be surprised though. I see plenty of people come through here doing the walk who aren't climbing the mountain.'

'Idiots.' I shake my head knowingly.

'Aye, makes no sense to me.'

After no more than an hour propping up the bar, the exertions of the day well and truly catch up with me. I say my goodbyes and slump off back to my cabin. It's got distinctly chilly whilst I've been dining and I immediately switch on the electric heater. This succeeds in filling the room with the whiff of burning dust, without appearing to emit any actual heat. Unperturbed I lie down on the bed to write up some notes from the day. I also take the opportunity to send everyone I know a picture of my red-raw and bite-strewn ankles. I feel it's important that the folks back home don't become indifferent to the extreme levels of danger and challenge I'm facing out here in the wilderness. Not to mention the out-and-out heroism I'm displaying with every step. I decide not to mention that I won't be camping tonight, or indeed ever again, even in the event of Hell freezing over.

DAY FOUR

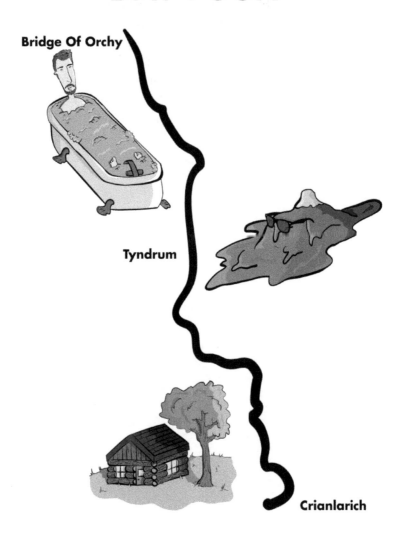

Bridge Of Orchy

Tyndrum

Crianlarich

Day 4: Crianlarich to Bridge of Orchy

Storm Clouds, Local Cuisine &
Less Than the Price of a Vacuum Cleaner

Strawberry – no wait – bana... No, strawberry. I gulp down my breakfast (which isn't in the least bit curdled, so hopefully only one of the holy beverages has been spoiled. Hurrah!) and contemplate leaving the cosy comfort of the bed to face another day. I've slept for a lengthy ten hours and as a result I'm feeling more than a touch fuzzy-headed this morning. The sun is already streaming through the curtains and the cabin is a good deal warmer than it was last night. Once I've conjured up a dash of the famous Reynolds get-up-and-go spirit and am duly setting about the morning prep (taking special care re direction of trouser) I notice that the bites covering my feet and ankles appear to have spread somewhat overnight. I've been scratching absentmindedly since awakening and can now see that my lower back, arms and even neck are all displaying their fair share of the small itchy lumps. Only one conclusion can reasonably be drawn from this as far as I can see. Some of the dreaded stowaways have decided to flee the infected tent and are on the move.

After allowing the grey matter a few moments to really chew things over re coming up with a potential plan of action, it is with great regret I must report to you that it fails me utterly in this time of need. The first few bars of Quantum Leap begin to sound, but I abruptly push them aside... 'No, brain! There'll be none of that - pull yourself together. We need to think this thing through right now for both our sakes.' I can't actually see any of the blighters. (And have no intention of unpacking the tent). I have no access to a washing machine and, thanks to A. Walker, I have no insect repellent. You may argue, dear reader, that to the best of your recollections A. Walker only suggested an (effective) alternative protection against midges and that if I didn't bring any insect repellent it's probably my own bally fault, all things considered. Well perhaps, although I don't actually recall asking you your opinion on the matter. I mean if you're going to side with A. Walker at the drop of a hat, without even a thought for the feelings of your faithful narrator, then I fear for our future relationship prospects, dearest reader, I really do. There I've said it. Anyway; to cut a long and hopeless story short; I eventually reach the same conclusion as the old brain viz; there's nothing to be done. I boldly venture forth to greet the day, scratching heartily as I go, covered in a shiny layer of Avon SSS and with trousers pointing in the correct direction.

The day's walk to Bridge of Orchy begins with the long haul back through the still deserted streets of Crianlarich. Eventually I locate the path I trod yesterday, which will take me steeply uphill back through the woods to rejoin the trail proper. This turns out to be exactly what was required in order to re-introduce a splash of much-needed pep into the attitude of yours truly. The long and unyielding climb through the moss-covered woodland banishes all thoughts of damage done by my unwanted, tiny and ravenous travelling companions. The morning light flooding through the foliage gives the place a brighter and more colourful impression than it had the previous afternoon, and your narrator is in good spirits as he continues to climb upwards. Mr B. instructs me that I'm to remain in the woodlands for a good few miles yet, as once I pick up the West

Highland Way it will continue to forge its way through this huge area of forest.

When I do eventually reach the crossroads that link back up with the trail, I'm treated to a spectacular view of the mighty Ben More, that I'd somehow managed to miss in my tired state yesterday. Giant storm clouds have gathered above the vast and conical mountain and now completely engulf and obscure its peak. Ben More literally translated means 'great mountain' and that seems like a thoroughly apt appellation to me. (Alliteration *and* a clever word. Growth and Maturity, dear reader, growth and maturity.) It's the first time I've really looked at the old boy and he really does take the breath away. A jagged mass of vivid green and rocky silver rising up into the heavens. I'm struck by an overwhelming desire to climb the thing, but it's not to be. I force myself to end my wide-eyed appraisal and follow the trail back down into the woods.

I'm only plunged into the darkness temporarily however as within a few minutes I'm strolling along a heather-covered hillside, with impressive views of the ever-present River Fillan in the distance. The path continues likes this for a while: undulating gently up and down and alternating between open hillside and tree cover. I'm never actually leaving the forest as these open stretches are contained within it and continue to provide a feast for the old eyes as well as refreshing respite from the atmospheric gloom of the woods. I'm passing the by-now-familiar sight of wild campers to the sides of the path. As I'm a bit later this morning the folks I'm passing now are, for the most part, in the process of packing up to begin their days hike. I note with a smidgen of green-eyed envy that they don't seem to be struggling with this task. Adept folds are engineered into their canvas abodes with speed and skill before they're effortlessly popped back into their carry bags. All the carry bags curiously seem not to have shrunk during the night and accept the tents plus any appendages cheerily, as though welcoming home an old friend.

I fear I may be on the verge of something of an identity crisis, dear reader. You think you've found your true calling in life, you've even re-arranged your entire life around said calling. Reduced your working hours, impoverished yourself and dealt with many a raised eyebrow as a result. 'You're going part-time at work in your late thirties so that you can spend more time... *walking*?' Truth be told I've always struggled with the camping element. The hike itself gives me freedom, joy and unapparelled fulfilment – but the blasted tent brings me nothing but misery. I discovered my passion for hiking as a result of suffering from insomnia. It began as a kind of self-prescribed therapy and then morphed into a life-affirming passion. The thing about the camping, you see, is that it brings back the ruddy insomnia. That's the nub of the thing, in a nutshell, cutting to the chase and so forth. The deafening silences of sleeplessness, the racing mind of the braindead zombie, the black stillness of the unrested soul. Hiking has rid me of these things, camping brings them back. 4am is not my friend, dear reader, and I've no desire to reacquaint myself with it. Yet I feel I must. For how can I truly give my life over to hiking – to experience the wilderness – the most remote corners of this land – if I need there to be a warm bed waiting for me at the end of each day? It's not very adventurer-like is it? The nomad en suite.

I'm pulled from my puddle of self-pity by the sight of a footbridge nestled at the bottom of the hillside I'm currently clambering down. It passes over a burn where the water froths and splashes over the shiny surfaces of the rocks below. It's a scene that I've already come to think of as quintessentially West Highland Way. I watch the water cascade beneath me with a smile on my face before moving on. The path now rises just as steeply up as it had careered downward only a moment prior. I climb the slippery track and begin to work up a sweat once again as the sound of the crashing waters of the burn behind me fade away. Mr B. is urging me to look upwards as these skies are usually home to many a graceful buzzard. As I do so I catch sight of something and for a glorious split-second believe it may be the elusive golden eagle. It's far too small however and I can't even be sure it's a buzzard as it disappears behind the treetops in a blink of an eye.

A bracing climb follows and the path then widens considerably. Above the trees the sky is still raging without ever actually erupting. This mixture of sweltering heat and dark angry skies now seem as much a part of the character of this trail as the jagged mountain peaks, deep dark woods and flowing rivers and lochs. The going underfoot becomes increasingly uneven and rocky as I begin to head downwards again. The sound of the road is just becoming audible when the path turns suddenly and abruptly away from it. After further descent I arrive at a picturesque stone railway viaduct. The grand old structure, part of the old Caledonian Railway, demands attention. I stand underneath staring up at it for a minute or two before lumbering on. Negotiating the viaduct has somehow brought me back in line with the road that I just turned away from.

Fortunately though I'm now walking along an old disused road that runs alongside the main carriageway – so the ambience remains pleasant enough. I pass through a short stretch of young woodland before crossing the road and following a track heading toward the River Fillan. This takes me through a boggy and muddy field with a sign on the gate that reads: 'Keep well right... Believe me!' Never one to ignore a warning sign I cautiously shuffle my way along the righthand edge of the field until I reach the gate on the other side. From here a short track leads to a wide wooden bridge crossing the river. I pause halfway across to gaze out along the winding river. It's another spectacular view in a trail bursting at the seams with them. The river, flanked on either side by rich dark green trees, flows its way off into the horizon where more mountains and hills nestle amongst the blackening clouds.

The walking is now flat and easy – which, as far as this hike is concerned, renders me a touch suspicious. Fearing some back-breaking climb, or even another ruddy ladder, is just around the corner – I plough tentatively on. My concerns are soon forgotten though as the path settles into a gentle stroll through farmland and rolling meadows. Eventually I'm lead to an ancient looking graveyard belonging to the Priory of St Fillan. Local Christians believe that this is the site of the chapel of St Fillan himself. St Fillan was an eighth century monk, credited with bringing Christianity to the remote Highland communities. The site was later turned into a priory by Robert the Bruce – adding to the rich historical links between this area and the great man himself. There is no sign of the priory today however, which helps to give the intact graveyard a spooky deserted atmosphere. Mind you I seem to be finding most things spooky and/or eerie during this hike – so you'd probably do well to ignore my opinion in this regard.

I continue along the comfortable dirt track until I reach a collection of farm buildings, where a thistle-adorned waymarker sends me left. From here the track ambles gently downwards back in the direction of the main road. Not a single drop of rain has fallen, yet the storm clouds above me are now blacker than any I can remember seeing. They resemble great dense plumes of soot blanketing the skies. The sun still somehow thwarts them by managing to radiate its heat through the blackness and maintain the unearthly contrast between the blistering temperatures and the wild stormy vistas. I cross over the road and drag The Albatross over a stile not wide enough to accommodate our combined width, to rejoin the track just as it itself rejoins the riverside. Before swinging the pack back up onto the shoulders, I pause for a much-needed swig of the good old H2O. Whilst reaching into the bag for my water bottle I discover a small bag of chilli flavoured peanuts that I can't remember ever purchasing and pop them delightedly into the trouser pocket. Small victories.

I wander contentedly along beside the water, looking all about me as I do so. Since passing under the viaduct a few miles back I have, almost unnoticed, been walking through a giant sprawling valley and now that I'm back on this side of the road and away from the cover of trees, it's really beginning to open up. Eventually I split from the river to enter a maze-like section of bush and woodland, where the path branches off erratically in different directions. I pass a decidedly pretty mini-waterfall as I negotiate my way through the shrubbery. After wandering aimlessly for a while I come across a sign that reads: 'The Lochan of the Lost Sword.' It overlooks a small area of water – which I assume is the foresaid lochan – which I assume means something along the lines of miniature loch. The sign tells the tale of Robert the Bruce, having just lost the battle of Dalrigh, instructing his army to throw all their weapons into the lochan. This included his own legendary claymore sword. Rumour has it that this mighty weapon lies beneath the water to this day.

The path then thins considerably as it continues to pick its way through the trees. The landscape briefly begins to open up again as the trees start to give each other a wider berth. In the distance there is the unmistakeable hum of humanity and I consult Mr B. to discover I'm approaching the village of Tyndrum. The path veers closer to the railway line to which the earlier viaduct belongs, and into more woodland in the form of a forest of pine trees. I spend a very enjoyable few minutes walking through the attractive pines accompanied by birdsong loud enough to momentarily drown out the approaching noise of the road and village beyond. Once through the pines I reach civilization and am greeted by the sight of a caravan park and, a little further along the path a railway station. It's a tad on the early side for luncheon, but I see no harm in a healthy spot of brunch and so begin to look around for a suitable pitstop - whilst the path winds its way into the village.

Tyndrum is famous for being the smallest place in the UK to have two separate railway stations. One that services the Fort William line and the other the Oban line. This is apparently because in times gone by rival train operators owned separate lines running through the area. I should probably confess that this is all coming from the knowledgeable pages of Mr B., plus the modern marvel that is the internet. If I'm being completely honest with you, dear reader old thing – and I feel you've earnt my honesty - S. Reynolds had failed to notice that there were two railway lines at all. Too busy adventuring no doubt. The village is also a popular tourist spot, thanks largely to the West Highland Way. For this reason, its main road is adorned with numerous attractive hotels and pubs. The path circumnavigates the main strip however and leads up to Clifton village; created in the eighteenth century to provide homes for the workers of nearby lead mines.

Once in Clifton village the path again crosses over the main road to arrive at a small post office and shop. Outside the entrance stands a weather-beaten wooden table with accompanying benches, currently being occupied by a healthy swarm of hikers. As far as brunch goes this certainly seems to be the hottest venue in town amongst my cagoule-clad brethren. I nod and smile hellos to several of the assembled ramblers on my way into the shop, including the German couple who dined in the same pub as me last night. Once inside I naturally head straight for the Irn-Bru display – which proudly dominates the drinks section, bathing the polished floors with a heavenly orange glow. I then decide on a

Tunnock's Caramel Log to accompany my beverage. Not to be confused with the delicious Tunnock's Caramel Wafers widely available on both sides of the border of course. Oh no, this is an entirely different product and one I've not tried before. Possibly a range not yet to reach good old England. In the spirit of growth and maturity that continues to characterise this adventure I embrace the native confectionary with zero hesitation. I consider it the duty of any true adventurer to broaden their own horizons and be open to all experience.

Once I've paid I head back outside to the seating area and notice, to my disappointment, that my fellow thick-socked explorers seem to be predominantly chowing down on fruit, bottled water and bags of (unflavoured) nuts. For shame! *Tourists*. With a pitying roll of the eyes I grab the last remaining section of bench and plonk myself down. After saying hello to the foresaid Germanic couple, I begin to get to work on my chosen brunch items whilst they get back to their conversation. For the second time in a few days I'm left to speculate on what might be being said.

'Don't look now, Sweetie-Pie, but I'm almost certain that the handsome fellow who just joined our table is that smash-hit indie author (note: that's a trendy way of saying self-published) S. Reynolds.'

'Ooh... Let's ask him to sign our copies of his book... That we of course carry around with us wherever we go.'

Or...

'Don't look now, My Snookum's but the funny little chap covered in bites who just joined our table is stuffing his face with chocolate bars and fizzy drinks!'

(Rolls eyes) 'What an amateur.'

Or...

I suppose there's an outside chance they weren't talking about me at all, as unlikely as I know that sounds. Well... Whatever the case, it continues to be a genuine pleasure to be sharing this trail with so many different nationalities. Like-minded souls from all across the globe assembling in this beautiful country in answer to the wild call of the Highlands.

I'm delighted to report that the caramel log is every bit as delish as its more widely-circulated wafer sibling. In fact, dear reader, may I suggest that you immediately begin a comprehensive media campaign to ensure it becomes more readily available south of the border. I would do so myself you understand – but I'm too busy being a fearless adventurer at present. If you could get that sorted in time for my return it would be appreciated. Once my snacks of choice have checked into their final place of rest - the belly of the noble S. Reynolds - I rise to my feet and reach for The Albatross.

The German couple are already disappearing into the distance by this point but a good few chomping ramblers remain huddled around the table and bench as I set off along the path again. The track once more takes the form of an old disused military road, which is an apt surface to allow brunch to settle as well as enabling me to complete a spot of pressing admin. I've neglected to book a room for the night and so proceed to do so via the app on my phone. The Bridge of Orchy Hotel is the only option open to me if I'm to finish the day in the location planned. It's therefore with fingers firmly crossed that I make the enquiry. As luck would have it there is but one room remaining – which I duly snap up. In doing so however I finally destroy any illusions of completing this trip on budget. The room sets me back... Well, I politely decline to divulge the exact figures, but rest assured it's more than I can afford and equates to the price of all accommodation up to this point combined... and then some.

As if my guilt at making such a lavish expenditure had somehow sprouted legs and ran home to tell on me, I receive a text message from Tasha at that exact moment. It's simply a 'Hi, how's it going?' enquiry but I briefly feel as though I've been caught drinking leftover gravy from the plates in the washing up pile. (If that seems like quite a specific example to have used... Well... In my defence, you've probably never tasted my Grandma's homemade gravy, have you? The woman is the Michael Schumacher of gravy making: relentless perfection. To waste it would have been unthinkable.) Besides, in truth Tasha isn't the slightest bit interested in what I spend my money on. When entering into a successful life partnership wherein one half of the union is known to regularly spend the majority of their monthly wage on rare and collectable Carter USM memorabilia – it is advisable to maintain separate bank balances. For the greater good. Not that Tasha's one to talk of course. I mean to say, dear reader, this is the woman who once spent £1,000 on a vacuum cleaner. That's right you heard me, one thousand pounds sterling... On a vacuum cleaner, by Jove! The cunning sales person appealed to my significant other's green credentials you see, dear reader. The blasted thing has a life-time guarantee – ergo more environmentally sound in the long run. It wouldn't be so bad if Tasha ever did any vacuuming. As already touched on; outmoded gender stereotypes are not observed in the Reynolds/Clarke household... That should probably be Clarke/Reynolds household. So it's muggins here lugging around the most expensive vacuum cleaner in the world, which – by the way – weighs roughly the same as a combine harvester. (Note to self: probably delete this bit for the 2nd draft... No sense in 'risking the wrath', so to speak.) I've veered off subject again haven't I? Anyway – hotel booked (for less than the price of a vacuum cleaner) and dearest love replied to – let's crack on.

I continue along the cobbled surface accompanied by the familiar sights and sounds of the main road, the railway line and a small flowing river, all sharing my direction of travel. After a few minutes an elderly but nonetheless chipper collie dog appears up ahead and saunters over to me with tail wagging. I make a fuss of the lovely old boy whilst his owners catch up. An aged couple with walking sticks, sensible socks and smiling faces soon arrive on the scene.

'Now, you see he's hoping you've got a bacon sandwich for him stowed away in your pocket,' says the fellow still smiling broadly and looking lovingly down at the mutt.

'Afraid not. Just some chilli nuts.'

Silence follows my reply and the faces of the walking-stick-clad couple cease their smiling and instead assume a look of confusion mixed with mild fear. Even the dog looks up at me questioningly. Realising what I've said I pull the bag of peanuts I'd found earlier from my pocket and hold them up for all to see, as if to say:

'Don't worry, I'm not a weirdo… Look, I have peanuts.'

After a few awkward seconds they visibly relax and we have a jolly good chinwag whilst the dog – named Dougal – takes a breather and sprawls himself out across the path.

After saying our goodbyes I'm continuing to stroll along the military road when I'm halted by the views sprawling out in front of me. This trail is yielding so many grand vistas and breath-taking sights that it's all too easy to become accustomed to them and even begin to take them for granted. For someone that still spends a large proportion of their time on this spinning rock sat in front of a computer screen this is foolhardy verging on criminal. Since leaving Clifton village behind, the scene around me has been quietly opening up and becoming gradually more spectacular. The path is sat just off centre at the base of a valley. To the left, behind the road, the hillside rises up into the clouds under the cover of trees. To the right, beyond the railway line, trees are again densely adorning the steep hillside but just up ahead I can see them give way to harsh and unforgiving moorland. The scale of the scene is what is most arresting. I feel as though Rick Moranis has miniaturised me with his homemade shrink ray machine (Oh come on people, everyone's seen '*Honey I Shrunk the Kids*', right? *Surely?*). This glorious vision seems to have no horizon, it stretches lazily off into infinity. Indeed, Mr B. confirms I'll be remaining in the valley all the way to Bridge of Orchy – news which I greet with a hearty smile.

I reach a small arched bridge that crosses the river and then almost immediately a second that takes me over the railway line. A short climb follows as the path re-establishes itself slightly higher up the righthand side of the valley. In the distance up ahead, I can see the German couple from earlier. After briefly marvelling at the prospect of actually catching up and passing someone (a rarity for your enthusiastic but bumbling narrator), I begin to ponder the strange relationship that you have with those around you when walking a long-distance trail. I consider myself to be a relatively amiable chap and thus can often be found engaging in chitchat with fellow wanderers – although in truth it usually needs to be the other party that gets the ball rolling so to speak. Naturally though there will be many folks that you'll simply nod to in passing. So what's the established protocol if you keep seeing those same folks? That's not a rhetorical question reader – I need an answer from you. Take these two for instance. This will be the third time we've run into each other over the last day or so, so what's the etiquette? Is it like a third date in that I now need to make my move? Um... actually scrap that comparison... Sounds a bit creepy when I see it written down – but you get the gist of the thing.

In the end, once I do catch them up, we simply smile and say hello for a third time. It appears they are forever destined to be 'The German Couple' in my own story. I wonder what I'm called in theirs? 'The Shiny Skin Man', 'Big Bag Man' perhaps 'The Irn-Bru Kid.' Actually, I like that one. T' clouds continue to rumble overhead and the e? heat is getting closer and stickier. Up ahead

Beinn Odhar looms into view. Its distinctive rounded peak with an off-centre cone-shaped point plonked on top of it instantly reminds me of my favourite hill back home. Crook's Peak sits in the Mendip Hills not too far from Bristol and, although it's a baby when compared to Beinn Odhar, the silhouettes they cast are strikingly similar. As a result, I feel an instant affinity toward it and am once again struck by the urge to climb it. If I could be so bold as to make one recommendation to anyone considering walking this trail; it would be to book a few days longer than you need. This will enable you to explore some of the stunning mountains that make up so much of the views along the way.

I reach a crossroads of tracks where I temporarily depart from the military road to again climb slightly further up the hillside. After a few minutes this new track descends again and I'm taken underneath the railway line, shortly after which I rejoin the old military road once more. From above it must appear as though the railway and the trail are locked in a tangled embrace as they dance their way through the rugged landscape. The road has disappeared somewhere off to the left and this, combined with the abrupt ending of the forest that's been by my side since Tyndrum, gives the valley an even greater sense of desolate drama. A few hundred yards further along a new river appears to the left, as if drafted in to replace the road, and weaves along snake-like and seductive beside the track. As I plod along I realise I'm repeating the line 'Cheese, glorious cheese, cold water and Mars Bars' over and over again under my breath. Which I'm thinking is probably a subtle hint from my subconscious that a spot of lunch might be in order. Long-term I probably need to think about reining in the audible mantra earworm nonsense a touch. As the path begins to curve round to the right and the huge Beinn Dorain appears up ahead I find a spot by the river and reach for my lunch rations.

Whilst munching on a processed stringy cheese snack I continue to look up at the grand old mountain. It's as vast as any but it gets there in a different way somehow. It's a far wider landmass than any I've seen thus far. Its width and less urgent gradient combine to give it a kind of melted appearance. As though you've left your mountain in the sun for too long and it's collapsed. Or perhaps it's more accurate to describe it as a lazy quality. As though it's slouching down on the sofa at the end of a hard day to watch re-runs of Have I Got News for You on Dave. I feel sympathy for the old chap. It must get a tad laborious standing to attention for all eternity, having to be all grandiose all the time. Do you know, dear reader, I'm not sure that processed stringy cheese snacks are wholly adequate as a main luncheon component? I seem to be just as hungry once I've consumed the things as I was before I started. I mull this over as I'm wolfing down my chocolatey second course. Once finished I creak to my feet, don the pack and begin the short three or so miles to my final destination for the day.

Afternoon

I continue to amble on along the path heading towards the foot of Beinn Dorain. The river flowing beside me soon encounters another, the mightier Allt-Kinglass, travelling across it in the other direction from left to right. The latter mercilessly gobbles up the unsuspecting former. A few yards from the point where the two rivers collide I'm greeted by the sight of another bridge. A slightly ramshackle stone arch that has a refreshingly unpretentious simplicity about it. I'm rather taken by it and scan Mr B. to see if there's any interesting historical nuggets connected to it – only to find, to my consternation, that he callously dismisses it as being of 'rather crude construction'. We can't agree on everything I suppose, beauty is in the eye of the beholder and all that. Still, as I set about crossing the aforementioned bone of contention I feel a certain cooling in my hitherto unwavering regard towards my sage travelling companion. Immediately after the bridge the path turns sharply left and I'm required to clamber over a stile, which very nearly sees me fall to my death. Well... To a bruised posterior at the very least.

The going remains easy despite the path now beginning to gently rise upwards. The leisurely nature of the walking continues to be in contrast to the ever-wilder landscape around me. 'A true taste of Highland grandeur' is how Mr B. describes this stretch (in a transparent attempt, I feel certain, to win back my adoration). The left turn means I'm now walking along the foot of Beinn Dorain. The path seems to have been carved into the base of the mountain itself. To my right a continuous sheer exposed rockface creates a wall between me and the hillside. Mini waterfalls beautify the wall in several places, splashing water onto the path. By way of confirmation that I'm nearing the hotel; more and more people are passing me by, as the sun breaks through the clouds for the first time in what feels like an age. Families out for a hike with the kids and faithful pooch in tow pepper the path in both directions.

The trail then crosses the railway line one more time for good luck. One last embrace before the music stops. The last mile or so sees the return of clusters of thick forest in the far distance to my left. The road too winds its way back into view. The clouds are now on the brink of giving up the ghost altogether and the sun shines victorious on all who traverse the West Highland Way. Despite my comparatively late start this morning it's still only mid-afternoon, so it's at a distinctly leisurely pace that I make my way towards the finish line. It's been a great day's walking and I want to make sure I soak up every last morsel of foresaid Highland grandeur that this valley cares to yield. Eventually the path begins a mild descent as it veers gently left and I can see the Bridge of Orchy up ahead.

The Bridge of Orchy is a small village dominated by the hotel in which I'm to lay my head tonight. A large and indeed somewhat grand-looking white building sat on the much aforementioned road. (Which, for the dedicated road enthusiasts amongst you, I'm happy to confirm is the A82... so now you know.) The hotel is surrounded by a smattering of smaller white buildings and from my current vantage point the ensemble looks endearingly like a family of houses; or a mother with her young if you will. Behind the buildings runs the River Orchy, which even from here I can see is a far grander and more rambunctious body of water than any I've seen today. I can also see the bridge that gives the village its name and it's not one that I fancy Mr B. is likely to dismiss as being of crude construction. The stone bridge was built in the 16th century to aid the swift moving of troops around the remote and largely uninhabited Highlands. This was in response to the Jacobite uprisings of that century and formed part of a Highland-wide government initiative of bridge and road building to make travelling across this roughest of terrains possible.

It's strange and discomforting to comprehend that so much of the path I've trod up to now, not to mention the bridges I've crossed, were originally installed for the purposes of battle. It seems at first so abominable in the face of such staggering beauty. Yet – it also somehow grotesquely fits in with the harsh nature of this landscape. That blood should have been shed during the history of this remote and unforgiving wilderness seems almost a given. Its beauty is not tranquil, its stillness not quiet. The twin mountains of Beinn Dorain and Beinn an Dothaidh that cast their eternal shadow over this particular patch of rough country have no doubt claimed many lives themselves across the annals of time. The jaw-dropping and life-affirming wonder of the Highlands cannot be denied – but neither can its power or brutality.

I wander past the train station, pondering briefly as I do so the continued wealth of transport links enjoyed by each of the tiny isolated settlements that the trail has passed through. I cross over the road and head for the main hotel entrance. A large group of Scouts are gathered around the benches that sit out front of the building. I assume Scouts, although they seem perhaps a bit old to be so. They have the air about them of a group that's walked a long way and is now growing impatient waiting, one assumes, to be picked up by a mini-bus or suchlike and driven to a nearby campsite. Once through the door I'm greeted by the sight of a line at reception as long as a blue whale. One of the longer blue whales in fact, far from a standard length blue whale at any rate. I prop The Albatross up against a nearby chair and partake in that most British of pastimes; a good old spot of queuing.

Whilst whiling away the minutes I take note of the classy décor throughout the establishment. Mixing as it does the traditional period features of exposed dark woods and stone with a few sleek modern touches. I decide to ignore the odd mounted severed animal head staring down at me and begin instead to tune in to the conversations around me. The clientele is certainly of a more, shall we say, affluent strain that I'm perhaps accustomed to… But it strikes me that, just as with the previous locations I've stayed in over the last five days, everyone is a walker. I catch snippets of chat regards the day's jaunt and shared anecdotes from the miles already clocked, as well as thoughts on those still to come. Not for the first time I feel a pleasing sensation of being a part of something shared. Who knows, or indeed cares what any of these folks do back in the real world. Out here – we're all walkers, and we're all on the same journey. United by an unwavering desire to get out on the trail.

My room is a split-level extravagance with a grand four-poster bed and an unreasonably plush en suite bathroom. The television alone is bigger than my tent. I take the opportunity to indulge in the long overdue bain moussant (that's bubble bath in French... G & M people, G & M). It's whilst lounging amongst the opulent foamy waters that I call Tasha and the folks in turn. I recount stories of wild and grandiose vistas to my Pops, tales of stormy derring-do to Tasha and confirmation of adequate toilet facilities and friendly old sheepdogs called Dougal to Mumsy dearest. All of them get to hear about my brave embracing of new cultures vis-à-vis my sampling of the local cuisine at brunch. None of them get to hear a jot regards the cost of tonight's accommodation.

Next on the agenda from amidst my bubbly citadel is a spot of bite inspection. Some progress has been made in this area I'm pleased to report. Where once there were unsightly patches of inflamed red skin, dotted with maddeningly itchy protuberances – now lie perfectly normal looking skin, dotted with maddeningly itchy protuberances. I glance over at my badly packed tent in its misshapen carry-bag. 'I know you're still in there, you little blighters... Whatever it is you're planning you can forget it right now... Fool S. Reynolds once; shame on you, fool S. Reynolds twice...' My thoughts are interrupted as my relaxed state causes me to inadvertently pass wind and I become briefly distracted, watching as the soapy bubbles are joined by a small eruption of new ones. Soon after this I notice that everything's getting a bit wrinkly and prune-like and decide it's probably time to get dressed and go downstairs for a spot of well-earned dinner.

In the disheartening absence of pizza, I plump for the only vegetarian option on the menu; wild mushroom gnocchi, which is perfectly pleasant. I then wander to the bar area and indulge in a few single malts. This is precursed by another conversation wherein I need to bluff my way around the whisky collection –

although in fairness, I can definitely now confirm that I'm firmly lodged in the oak cask camp, rather than the sherry. Smoky and peaty are my preferred undertones. I can see that doesn't sound any less plonkerish written down than it does spoken out loud. Good to know. Just as I'm starting to consider retiring for the evening the German couple appear at the bar. The woman looks over and smiles at me as she says,

'Hello again. We've been seeing a lot of you, haven't we?'

We then finally get to have a proper introduction and proceed to spend a few minutes swapping stories from the walk so far. Their names are Clara and Henri and they're also walking the whole trail, including Ben Nevis. It's a hike that they've wanted to take for many years and they're clearly loving every minute of it. They clock a few bites on my arms and seem a touch amused as I attempt to explain why it is that I'm using a beauty product instead of insect repellent.

'Would you like to have our spare bottle?'

'No, no... This is legitimately proven... The marines use it... So... y'know.'

Eventually we wish each other all the best for the rest of the trail and I make my way back up to my room. I spend the rest of the evening lying in bed watching a forgettable movie and writing up some notes regards today's walk. A long hike to Kinlochleven awaits tomorrow and I'm brimming with excitement to get back out there.

DAY FIVE

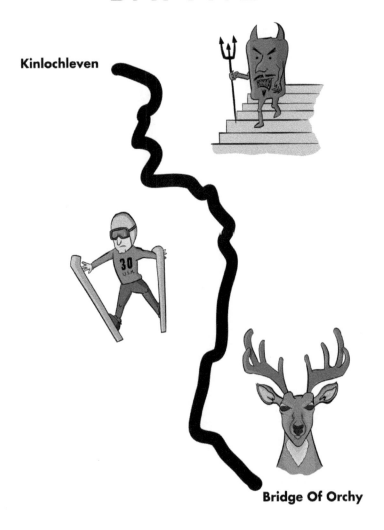

Kinlochleven

Bridge Of Orchy

Day 5: Bridge of Orchy to Kinlochleven

A Moment of Clarity, Ski Resorts
& The Devil's Staircase

It's somewhere between 5 and 6am the following morning and I'm staring out of my bedroom window watching the sunrise over the Bridge of Orchy. I'd only got up to use the bathroom but the orange glow seeping into the room from behind the curtains was too enticing to be ignored. Well let's be honest, I'm not going to get back to sleep now am I, dear reader? May as well begin the morning ablutions and get out there as soon as possible I say. Once ready to go I reach into the bag for a strawberry Weetabix drink – never before has such a clear-cut strawberry day presented itself to me. Unfortunately - to my horror - it soon becomes all too apparent that I'm clean out of strawberry-flavoured beverages. It's banana from here on in. 'Faint heart never won fair lady,' I mutter to myself, unsure exactly what I mean by it, as I crack open the liquid breakfast and swig it down.

Almost immediately upon leaving the hotel I'm crossing over the village's eponymous bridge and looking out along the sparkling surface of the river. I'm now shrouded in daylight but the manner in which the water shimmers reflectively up at me still has something of the pale moonlit glow about it. The path then diverges from the road and leads me upwards into the trees that flank one side of the village. The uphill slog is initially not a particularly steep one but it's enough to wake the

89

old leg muscles from their slumber. I'm moving at pace this morning as well; partly because it's a long walk ahead and a spot of early progress wouldn't go a miss. But mainly because I'm eager to get out onto the boggy isolation of Rannoch Moor. If I was required to disclose my favoured landscape re putting stout foot to trusted floor, I would undoubtedly describe myself first and foremost as a coastal walker. There's something about the sea that never fails to reach inside of me and give the soul a ruddy good old enriching. That being said, as the months have passed and I've continued to explore my passion for hiking; I wouldn't hesitate to place the wild open spaces of moorland walking a very close second. Whether it be discovering the forgotten paths of Exmoor with my Pops or climbing the ancient Tors of Dartmoor – the immense exposed moorland landscape never fails to deliver an addictive impression of true freedom and wildness.

The path has taken the form of a wide dirt track that continues to forge a straight and true course through the tall pine tree plantations on either side of it. The gradient is becoming a tad punchier and soon causes my pace to slow somewhat. Above me the sun and several brooding ominous storm clouds are picking up where they left off yesterday, in the battle for dominance of the early morning skies. Eventually I'm clear of the forest and the path zigzags left and right as it continues to climb. The views behind me are opening up as I begin to rise above the treeline - but I'm focussed on the crest of the hill that lies tantalising up ahead. I courageously puff my way along the final few hundred yards to reach the summit... And then I see it.

Every good trail has its moments. Those views or stretches of journey that burn themselves into your memory. Images to draw strength from in future times of need. This trail has undoubtedly already delivered admirably in that regard. The first sight of Loch Lomond in all its majesty from atop Conic

Hill being the image that leaps to mind. I've come to understand though that the very best of trails, the absolute corkers I mean, are those which yield one single moment that transcends even those most memorable of highlights. A moment that is *more* than spiritually uplifting or eye-wateringly beautiful.

The view before me now is of a single track winding its way downward across Rannoch Moor and ever onwards to the unreachable horizon beyond. Mighty mountain peaks intensely survey the scene from all sides like eternal watchmen. The sky is erupting above as shades of pink and orange fill the gaps left by the raging clouds of black and grey. The surface of Loch Tulla emanates an unearthly blue glow that breaks the dark green carpet of the moor. A single tree stands alone and defiant beside a cairn. Forever braced against the oncoming storm, bloodied but unbowed. In the far distance a small group of red deer turn at the sight of me and head gracefully back towards the horizon. All save for the stag, who stands tall to face me for a brief moment from across the savage landscape. From this distance he is no more than a silhouette, but a noble and striking one. His proud and jagged antlers are the crown in his kingly pose. After a moment he turns and follows his pack... But in his own time and on his own terms. The wind is a ceaseless deafening howl in which all life is imprisoned. And in this life affirming scene, dear reader, everything suddenly makes sense again and my brief identity crisis is at an end.

I am not an adrenaline junkie, nor do I desire to be. I'm no more suited to the career of a survivalist than I am that of a high-powered businessman. What I am is a bumbling and contented rambler. I wander... therefore I am. Moments like this are the reason I do what I do. Moments like this are also the reason why the decisions I've taken to re-arrange my life, in order to spend as much of it as possible hiking, are the correct decisions. For me. It may not make sense to some, but then that's life I suppose. We're each of us different and the only point to any of this as far as yours truly can fathom (if you don't mind taking a spot of existential advice from a man who only 48 hours ago was wearing his trousers back-to-front) is to find out what makes you happy and, as long it doesn't hurt anyone else, do everything you can to grab it. It's true to say that whilst some others are sleeping or sitting in front of a computer screen you might well find me out in some remotest of spots, in all weathers, following some forgotten trail or other (and looking pretty dashed heroic whilst doing so no doubt). But It's also true to say that whilst some others are scaling mountain peaks and wrestling wolves to the ground you might well find me at the hotel bar pretending to know about whisky or passing wind in a giant bubble bath. Hurrah for the nomad en suite! It's then that the clouds erupt and the rain finally comes. Still standing at the summit of the hill I lift my face upwards and let tears from heaven wash away my own.

Crikey! – Still with me, old thing? All getting a touch hysterical what! – Let's apply the stiff upper lip and carry on, shall we? I march onwards into the rain and wind with a sense of joie de vivre that's been at least partially missing since waking up at 3am in a tent on the banks of Loch Lomond. The path continues to zig-zag downwards into the wildness of Rannoch Moor as the herd of deer keep a watchful eye on my progress from afar. I pull the hood of my raincoat tight around my head, which simultaneously blocks out layers of sound whilst intensifying the noise of the rain, as though I were hearing it from beneath a sheet of corrugated plastic. Not for the first time I find myself inadvertently picking up the pace when I get to a stretch of trail that I don't want to end. I've wondered for a while now if this contradictory and involuntary action is peculiar to me or whether all walkers catch themselves doing it from time to time. The excitement and exhilaration of the trail at its very best, no doubt. In any case, I force myself to slow down and revel some more in my surroundings.

After a short while the Inveroran Hotel becomes visible up ahead, as does the small road that links it to civilization. The trail joins the road to navigate its way around the hotel, which although not as grand as its counterpart in the Bridge of Orchy, nonetheless emanates a warm and enticing country pub vibe as I saunter cheerily past. Continuing to follow the road, I then cross over a river and am greeted by the familiar sight of wild campers, pitched along its bank. Well over a dozen colourful tents whose (mostly sleeping) inhabitants clearly also picked up on the alluring country pub ambiance of the nearby hotel. A couple of fellow early morning types are packing up their tent and getting ready for the off. Upon seeing me they both give me hearty waves and fresh-faced smiles that would swell even the most shrivelled of cardiac wotsits. I duly return the gesture and carry on with a spring in the step as the road swings round to the right.

Either side of the road the moor is becoming marshier and the ground between me and Loch Tulla is covered with large puddles of murky water. The rain has died down to a spray that's too light to penetrate the wind and so swirls around in the air, as if propelled by an invisible garden sprinkler. Tall pine trees huddle together for warmth and protection in small groups that sporadically speckle the landscape. I reach a bridge named Victoria, which kindly grants me safe passage over another flowing river. Beyond the bridge lies a building that Mr B. advises me is called Forest Lodge and it is here that the path leaves the road behind. The track is now rougher underfoot but still clearly defined as it winds its way onward towards a much larger area of pine trees.

I'm walking slightly uphill again as I pass along the edge of the woodland. I look deep into its black abyss at rows of straight tree-trunks that gradually fade from view as the darkness swallows them. It's strange that something so obviously manmade and with a uniformity so seemingly at odds with the open moor on which it stands, should feel so much a part of this landscape. I travelled the length of our island to be here amongst the remote emptiness of the moors and the savage beauty of the mountains – but these atmospheric plantations have been integral to my Highland experience thus far. As if reading my thoughts, the woods come to an abrupt end and the wilderness reclaims its territory. It's another goosebumps moment, yet I fear I may have run out of superlatives, dear reader. Peaked too soon with all that oncoming storm and rain from heaven stuff, eh?

Let me then put it this way, if I may? One of my oldest and dearest chums is a stout fellow named M.J. Botting. Once, when we were in primary school (M.J. Botting and your very own S. Reynolds were a pretty big deal in Barnham County Primary back in the day, but that's a story for another time), foresaid MJB was using the lavatory. There he was minding his own biz, sat atop the throne with trousers down, when who should burst into the cubicle but Vicky McBride! (Vicky was the school sweetheart upon whom we all doted shamelessly. Actually, I should probably make up a fake name for her, shouldn't I? Protect the innocent and all that. Let's call her... Vi... Actually I just need to type it straight over that last bit, don't I... Hang on, I'll do that now... OK, Done). Anyway, Vicky marches straight in, bold as brass, looks at the young M.J., mid... whatnots, and proclaims 'Malcolm, I love you'. Now I don't know if in real life this proclamation was immediately followed by the sound of a gentle splash as plop hits water, but for the sake of comedic value let's say that it was. In any case the point I'm making is that the emotions felt by the six-year-old M.J. Botting as he sat wide-eyed upon the toilet that fateful day are similar to those that I feel now, as I stand looking out over the splendour of Rannoch Moor. The sense one has when truly comprehending for the first time in one's life that, all things considered, the world is an utterly tiptop place.

As I continue along the uneven cobbled track I start to wonder how on earth the thing was ever built in the first place. As well as huge waterlogged patches of ground the moor is covered in black void-like deposits of thick peat. They lie in wait amongst the clumps of heather and standing water for any traveller foolhardy enough to wander from the path. The complexities, sheer hard work and determination required to build anything in these conditions is more than my pampered mind is able to comprehend. Astonishingly I'm still passing the odd stubborn tree standing isolated amidst the desolation. The rain has now stopped and the sun is shining down brilliantly through the gaps in the clouds. Its rays are causing every surface of water to reflect the sky above and turning the landscape into a battlefield of light versus dark. An echo of the sun's own fight against the huge dark clouds, which still rages on up above.

Up ahead I see a fellow rambler and briefly consider where it is she has come from for us to be crossing paths on this stretch of moor at this time of the morning. A hardier soul than myself who's pitched the canvas out here in the wilds, I suppose. We're then trapped in that slightly peculiar scenario that all walkers find themselves in on occasion. The only two people in a vast deserted landscape slowly walking towards each other from a great distance. The temptation is to outstretch the arms and run towards them in slow motion as if in a scene from a romantic movie… Or perhaps that's just me? When we eventually reach each other, we stop and say hello. The fact that she's soaked through and shivering seems to initially suggest I may have been correct in assuming she's spent the night on the rainy Rannoch Moor, but the fact she's only carrying a daypack suggests otherwise. Despite her bedraggled appearance she's buzzing with the energy of this place. How could you not be?

'I'm pleased to see you, as it means I'm not the only one crazy enough to be out in this,' she says with a grin and a thick Irish accent.

'Ha, yeah. There's at least two of us at any rate.'

Her name is Sarah and she's actually staying at the Inveroran Hotel. She's on her way back there now, after going out for an early morning hike. She tells me that she's definitely going to be doing the whole trail in future, having immensely enjoyed the last few days holidaying here. We say our goodbyes and slowly walk away from each other... Two moving dots on a vast open landscape, travelling in opposite directions.

Eventually the path levels off and reveals yet more incredible views. The mighty twin peaks of Black Mount dominate the scene as I head towards a small bridge that crosses a stream and directs the path alongside to another area of woodland. This provides shelter from the winds, although in truth they are beginning to die down as the sun strengthens its grip on the day. A bird emerges from above the treetops and flies by overhead. Not a golden eagle, dear reader... Woe is me. But now that I'm looking at it I can see it's definitely a bird of prey, the right size to be a kestrel, but silhouetted against the sun as it is, it's impossible to make out. The research that I've done (oh be quiet, I can do research... You don't know that I haven't) before taking this trip has told me that Rannoch is full of exciting wildlife. As well as being one of the spots where you're most likely to catch sight of the golden eagle you can also hope to see roe and red deer, red squirrel and that most elusive of creatures; the wildcat. Although I'm starting to begrudgingly accept the possibility that I won't ever get to gaze upon the golden eagle, I cannot bring myself to be too disappointed at this particular moment.

The sight of the red stag earlier this morning is one that will be with me for ever more.

I've come to realise that it's so often the case that the most desolate-seeming locations are in fact those most thriving with wildlife. I can regularly be found exploring the Quantock Hills in Somerset, for whom I have a love bordering on obsession. They are in many respects like a mini-moor. With heather covered hills, forest adorned valleys and wild deer running free. They too have that beautiful and impossible contrast of at once being serene and empty yet also alive with the buzz and cry of all manner of life. Nowhere I've been thus far quite epitomizes this like Rannoch Moor though, dear reader. I'm finding myself stopping at increasingly regular intervals now, to stand and simply let the sights and sounds of the place engulf me.

I'm almost in a daze as I pass a third patch of plantation woodland. The moorland floor around me seems to be becoming even wilder the further I progress. One could lose track of time here, or even the very notion of it... For this landscape is eternal. I assume that every long-distance walker has in them somewhere a need for solitude? This may be wrong; for some I know hiking is a joyous communal affair. Many of the folks I've been lucky enough to meet along the way on this particular hike are testimony to that. But even so, as a breed I think it's fair to say that we crave an escape from modern life. A peace and, certainly in my own case, a solitude that simply cannot be obtained amidst the hue and cry of city life. If this is the case for you, dear reader, then go to Rannoch Moor immediately. Well actually finish this book first... Then go.

The path gradually starts to climb again as I pass a collection of ruins some way off to my left. Mr B. – whose tone, much like my own, has become more than a touch dramatized since we set foot upon the epic moor – describes them as the lonely ruins of Ba Cottage. Jeepers and furthermore a good dash of creepers, dearest reader... To have lived out here in total isolation with only nature's own fury for company. The mind boggles and all the hats one has ever owned are tipped in deference and respect to those most hardy and noble of spirits. As I contemplate such an existence the trail continues to ascend. I'm lead over numerous footbridges, crossing burns and streams that course through the landscape like pulsing veins. As I climb, the best of the views lie behind me and I find myself clumsily walking backwards up the hill so as not to miss out on a single moment of this magical place.

Eventually I reach a cairn that marks the summit of the hill. From here the trail heads left and more views open out in front of me. To a large degree this new panorama is a continuation of the breath-taking moorland scenery that has defined the day thus far. Two intruders upon the landscape mean this isn't completely the case however. The first of these is the pesky A82, which re-emerges to continue its speedy excursion through the Highlands. The second is a large, imposing building sitting alone some way back from the road. It looks as though someone may have erected it in this location by mistake. As though there may have been an awkward phone call upon its completion along the lines of:

'What do you mean, it's done? I'm here in Glasgow looking right at the Highland Way industrial estate and I ain't seeing squat Sonny Jim'.

'Wait... You're whe...? What did you just say'?

Not that I'm complaining, you understand. For also in view are numerous splendid mountain peaks, including those of Glencoe. These are some of the most beautiful yet and I'm pleased to note that the old spine is far from tingled-out as I gaze in awe at the magnificent old beasts. As the path winds its way back down the hill a few things become apparent. I see a second, much older, building sat just in front of the larger modern one. This turns out to be the still intact Blackrock Cottage and its presence somehow adds to the mirage-like absurdity of its immediate neighbour. I imagine a disbelieving highlander glancing up from his porridge oats (he has a big red bushy beard and is dressed from head to foot in tartan... My imagination apparently isn't up to much) to see that the view from his window has changed from remote wilderness to large ski resort. For a ski resort it is – and in fairness the closer I get to it the less it looks like the monstrous blot on the vista it first appeared to be.

It's actually got something of the large Swiss chalet vibe about it. It's also a complex rather than a single building and as I get even closer I can see that there's a ski lift running from it back up the hill just across from me. This comes as something of a shock and stirs the old grey matter into action. I suddenly realise that this whole landscape spends much of the year covered in snow. This may be all too obvious to you, dear reader. Indeed, while we're at it - it may also be obvious to you that processed stringy cheese things don't provide adequate nutrition when walking 20 miles a day. I should think it's also obvious to you that if you're hiking in Scotland in July you're going to need to bring insect repellent with you and that if you've spent six months planning a long-distance hike you should probably think to check how many days you'll need to finish the thing. I'd expect the direction of your own trouser is a relatively obvious concept to you as well. Good for you. Unfortunately though, this is my story and so you're just going to have to accept that it is only now that this revelation occurs.

As I amble past first the resort and then the cottage, absentmindedly finishing off my chilli nuts as go, I contemplate this further. What an unfathomably wondrous thing this trail must be in the depth of winter. I think back to the places I've seen and re-imagine them all covered in a blanket of snow. I'm sorely lacking experience of snow-hiking and mean to address this as soon as possible. Two days on the Black Mountains in Wales back in February of this year are my only real taste of it so far. The snow fell thick and fast for the duration on that occasion and with inches of snow already on the ground my navigational skills were well and truly put to the test. It may shock you to hear therefore that I spent most of the two days walking in ever-increasing circles, having absolutely no idea where I was. I thoroughly enjoyed it though... Plus I built a pretty exceptional snowman as I recall. I mean professional competition standard when all is said and done.

I'm forcibly removed from my flight of fancy by the sound of a car speeding past on the road up ahead. The path has merged with an old track, used by the ski-resort, and I can see it winding its way across the road and into the rugged terrain beyond. As I cross the road I pass the surreal sight of a woman waiting at a bus stop. Not surreal in and of itself I hear you interject, yet mere moments ago I was strolling through the edge of the world – now here I am crossing the A82 outside a ski-resort, eating chilli nuts whilst a woman waits for the bus. The cone-shaped mountain of Buachaille Etive Mòr reveals itself once I've cleared the road and rejoined the track. I'm now walking towards the mouth of Glencoe; an area considered to be one of the most beautiful places in the UK, or anywhere else for that matter. My pace quickens in anticipation, although in the beauty stakes it's difficult to imagine how anything can compete with what I've already seen today.

The first thing that strikes me as I approach is the fierceness of the scene. The rain has long since ceased and the sun has been shining merrily on high. It seems nobody has thought to tell Glencoe this however. Dark, foreboding clouds obscure the peaks on either side of the narrow glen. The road, the River Coupall and indeed the track on which I tread all run straight into the black belly of the beast. They are swallowed up by a wall of cloudy darkness that appears backlit by some unseen source with ghostly consequences. The whole thing has an unnerving gates of hell ambiance to it. It's very cool. There's a small clump of conifer trees up ahead and as I approach them it becomes clear that they are obscuring from view the Kinghouse Hotel. Which looks like a pretty spot considering it's situated at the gates of hell. The last resting place before eternal damnation.

As I near the hotel people begin to appear in droves. The car park is full with cars, bikes and a couple of coaches. The building itself is very much in the mould of the Inveroran before it. It's stood in this spot for over 200 years and it wears its history well. A period property with white-washed walls and character a-plenty. In amongst the holidaying families and fellow ramblers, groups of cyclists gather round their steeds, deep in conversation. There is a buzz about the place and nobody can keep their eyes off the fearsome Glencoe. I somehow manage to display superhuman levels of willpower yet again, by resisting the temptation to stroll into the bar for an early snifter. I wave a hearty hello at a few of the bystanders – like a marathon runner waving to an adoring crowd who have travelled far to cheer him on. I consider grabbing a cyclist's water bottle and squeezing it over my head to complete the picture, but decide against it and continue to follow the track, leaving the crowds behind.

The path crosses a small bridge over a stream, where Mr B. reckons there lives a large trout population. I don't see a single one however – zilch, zip, nada. I'm not suggesting he's got that wrong of course. Just seems a bit odd is all I'm saying. I'm briefly heading away from the main road until the track turns sharply left and realigns itself with it. After a further few hundred yards marching bravely onwards into the stormy mountainous vista the trail suddenly splits from the track, which heads downwards to meet the road. A sole waymarker stands proudly upright adorned with an arrow pointing right

101

towards a stony path heading uphill. This new direction is short lived however and the path is soon once again travelling in the same direction as the main road – although it's now a more pleasant distance away from it.

I hear giggling coming from behind me and turn around to see a group of young girls with backpacks as large as my own positively bouncing along the path. I can't tell you how young they are exactly, as I've unfortunately reached that point in my own life where everyone under the age of about 22 suddenly looks like a child – but it's safe to assume I think, that they're in their teens. I stand aside to let them bounce past and we exchange cheerful greetings as they do so. Over the next few minutes or so as they gradually disappear off into the distance, I catch a few snippets of their conversation. Typical teenage stuff regards drinking and love interests interspersed with a few references to subjects completely alien to me such as Instagram or Taylor Swift. I think back to my own teenage years and feel a great deal of respect for the girls as I laugh out loud at the notion of my chums and I embarking on a 100-mile trek through the Scottish Highlands. Walking home from the pub at closing time was enough to put undue strain on the old lung capacity. I safely surmise that within the first 48 hours we'd have all be lost or dead... Or both.

As the trail gently careers back downwards towards the road the going underfoot becomes steadily trickier. Streams of water cascade down the hillside and the rocky surface of the path becomes slippery as a result. In due course the path reaches the roadside and nestles in alongside it for a spell. People again begin to appear en masse. On the road itself cyclists speed past enthusiastically amongst the motorists as they gaze wide-eyed from their car windows at the awesome scenery. Scores of walkers appear heading in the opposite direction to myself, emerging from a car park up ahead. I arrive at a lonely house painted white and set amongst some pine trees beside a stream.

The house sits on a corner where the road branches left and the trail, finally leaving it behind, heads right and uphill. It's a busy spot with cars parked on either side of the road and groups of hikers and cyclists heading off into the wilderness from all directions.

I decide it's about time to chow down on some good old luncheon and find a pretty spot along the bank of the stream, underneath a footbridge that carries the trail uphill towards the ominous sounding Devil's Staircase. I reach into the depths of The Albatross and pull out a couple of stringy cheeses. They've now been sat in the bag for the best part of a week and have taken on a decidedly floppy and squidgy quality. I fail miserably to muster anything approaching enthusiasm as I stare down at them with creased brow and eventually shove them back from whence they came. Time may yet prove beyond doubt that man cannot live on Mars Bars alone – until then however, I intend to have a jolly good stab at it. In keeping with the improbable rate at which the weather has been changing throughout this trip; the sun has again broken through the clouds to bathe the scene in warmth and light. Water flows serenely along the rocky stream and doesn't fall too far short of drowning out the sounds of the nearby road and car park in the process.

The whole scene is bordering on the idyllic and S. Reynolds is all-at-once so relaxed that the trusty boots even come off. As the tired feet enjoy a rare airing and I contemplate a second course of MB all seems assuredly well with the world. Then the midges arrive. Like drunken gate-crashers at a private party, intent on intimidation and destruction. Before I can blink the semi-visible ruffians of the insect world are in my hair, on my skin and clothes and of course all over the newly exposed feet and ankles – which, lest we forget, are still recovering from the last merciless attack. Perhaps this is a daring rescue attempt in respect of their fallen brethren still trapped in the prison of my packed away tent. In any case I leap to my feet, grab the boots and backpack and make my retreat – flailing about in a wholly undignified manner as I do so.

I try to appear cool and casual as I emerge, flustered, from my luncheon locale to rejoin the crowds beside the parking areas. I quickly survey the damage done. Definitely some bites upon the scalp and a few fresh ones around the already mottled ankles. That apart however I appear unscathed. Most of the scoundrels seem to have come-a-cropper in the thick veneer of Avon SSS that coats my now baby-soft skin. (The redemption of A. Walker is complete.) Many of the critters still lie there in fact, in their watery graves. I brush them off before lacing up the boots and reaching for the pack. I spy a steady stream of folk walking over the footbridge and follow them across to rejoin the trail as it heads for the aforementioned fiendish stairway.

Afternoon

As I begin the - initially steady - climb out of Glencoe I consider the sinister name given to the patch of trail I'm now heading toward. In my experience the prefix of 'Devil's' to a landmark or stretch of track usually means I'm about to see something dramatic. I've walked through or past many devil's mouths, points and even a frying pan... This is my first staircase however. In those previous instances what I found were dramatically shaped rocky landscapes, usually on a vast scale. If you used your imagination you could squint and see how the scene before you may resemble a hellish creatures mouth... Or their really big frying pan. The Devil's Staircase however was given its fearsome moniker by the soldiers that had to haul their assorted kit up it in times gone by. The name in this instance therefore is purely in reference to the severity of the climb. Which, truth be told, isn't really that severe. I mean to say I'm obviously not carrying tons of ammunition, guns and everything I need to survive on my back. My own Albatross holds no more than some smelly clothes, floppy processed cheese snacks and a tent full of starving insects – and Lord knows I've moaned enough about carrying that trifling load up to this point. So, it's all perspective, you understand?

The staircase is in fact a series of widening zig-zags up a hillside that reaches little more the 250 metres. As I begin the ascent I can see that the stream of people climbing it extends all the way to the summit. It's essentially a long moving queue. The scene calls to mind an old computer game I played as a child called Lemmings. I imagine everyone reaching the summit of the climb and then jumping calmly off a sheer rockface one at a time to their certain death. I distract myself from this somewhat grizzly train of thought by adapting the song *Devil's Haircut* by Beck in my head to pass the time. 'I've got a Devil's Staircase I need to climb'. I mean that won't mean much to you unless you're a Beck fan, dear reader. So you'll just have to take my word for it that it's very funny of me... Not to mention clever.

On one of the many turns from zig to zag I'm greeted by a sign that reads 'Food & drinks this way'. It's a strange sight out here (knowing as I do that I'm a long way yet from any town or village) and initially amuses... This amusement wears off soon enough however as I continue to pass similar signs at regular intervals as the climb continues. 'You keep saying that but where are these ruddy drinks?' After a while I convince myself that it's no more than a cruel joke and decide it best to cast aside any hopes of imminent refreshment. I pass a few people taking a breather, including one young couple on the verge of an argument. One doesn't like to eavesdrop you understand, so let's just say that the general gist of the thing is that when party A had suggested to party B that a stroll in the idyllic surroundings was in order, party B had not considered that said stroll would include a ruddy big hill. Furthermore; party A's insistence on striding onwards in the manner of some hideous striding thing whilst a struggling party B languishes behind is not doing a jot to improve the overall situ. In summary I conclude that Party A has grossly overestimated party B's desire to ascend foresaid ruddy hill and is therefore in for something of a rough time of things – just as soon as party B has regained the strength required to administer foresaid rough time.

Eventually I reach the summit, with a good deal more understanding regards the soldier's hellish choice of name than I had possessed at the bottom of the hill. It's as I get my breath back that I spy the tuck shop containing the much-promised food and drinks. A bright yellow tent full of Irn-Bru and Tunnock's Caramel Wafers. If I haven't said it before I'd like it put on record here and now that the noble people of this land are most definitely cut from a superior cloth. I put some coins in the honesty box and take a can and a wafer with immeasurable gratitude. I make my way through the crowds to stand next to the cairn that marks the summit and soak up the views in each direction. The view in front is not a far reaching one as the track careers off between the two peaks of Beinn Bheag and Stob Mhic Mhartuin. The one behind though is as sobering as it is majestic. The sight of Glencoe in all its splendour for what, I assume, will be the last time on this trip. Another milestone reached as I head into the latter stages of this incredible trail. The tedious old pessimist in me fears that this sight must surely mark the end of the best stretch of this walk. The chipper optimist in me pipes up however and points out that many miles of rugged Highland wilderness still stand between me and the end of the trail in Fort William. Whatever the truth I feel privileged to have experienced the raw beauty of Rannoch Moor and Glencoe.

I've only walked a minute or two from the cairn when the trail validates the plucky optimistic view of things to come by delivering the latest panorama with devastating showmanship. Miles of grassy wild country sprawl out in front of me as the path cuts a white line through the green landscape and speeds ever onwards. The eyes widen as I look out at the distant mountainous backdrop and spy the distinctive shape of the mightiest peak of them all. The granddaddy of the Highlands. The highest summit in all the kingdom. The iconic Ben Nevis. I swig back the last of the Irn-Bru and resist the temptation to beat my chest and make Tarzan noises. There are still quite a few people around after all. Instead I let out a small belch, tuck the empty can into a side pocket of The Albatross and begin the long seven-mile or so descent towards my final destination for the day; Kinlochleven.

The clouds begin to gather once more as I stride onwards and the sky regains a slightly unearthly pink and orange glow. The further I stroll the fewer people there are in view in either direction along the path. I note that those still on the trail are, without exception, all walking with poles. I've never used poles myself, although I'm unsure exactly why that is. One reason for using them of course is to keep the old blood flowing freely around the old arm region. I certainly get my fair share of the dreaded 'fat fingers' condition towards the end of a day's walking – usually leading me to march in an absurd manner with arms flying back and forth at double the rate of the legs. A routine that is probably more effective in ensuring I continue to be a solitary walker than it is at getting the claret swirling at will around the upper body. Perhaps it's time to invest in some new kit then?

With the exception of my boots (which cost more than my car – not that that means much to be honest with you – car and boots combined come to less than the price of our vacuum cleaner), I've never really invested too much re the quality of my walking gear. If I'm being totally honest with you, dear old things, I think I may even have a bit of a chip on the shoulder in that regard. Some kind of foolhardy reverse snobbery on my part. I think of long distance walking as a rejection of modern consumerism in some way – an escape from the rat-race. The shedding of all the 'stuff' that clogs up our existence and parades itself as the justification for the mundanity of our 9-to-5 culture. Interestingly I never seem to have these philosophical revelations when I'm sprawling out on a four-poster bed in a swanky hotel or supping on a single malt at the bar. Nevertheless, the long-distance trail is the only place on earth where I'm able to fully obtain what I crave from life. The simple and uncomplicated beauty of the world. Walk. Sleep. Repeat. Somehow the notion of shiny and expensive kit impinges on that simplicity.

I know, I know. Utterly absurd. Please don't assume I ever apply this misguided logic to my fellow ramblers. I reserve this nonsense for myself alone. It matters not a jot to me what those I share the trail with choose to adorn themselves in. No matter our surface differences - anyone, woman or man, who chooses to spend their time hiking in the wilderness is a brother or sister in all but blood. Well... a close cousin at any rate. Actually - maybe scrap the family metaphor... Sounds a bit creepy when I see it written down. I think the ultimate take away point here, dear reader, is that I should probably buy some walking poles.

After continuing to descend at a steady rate for a further fifteen minutes or so – during which time I maintain my incredulous wide-eyed and open-mouthed appreciation of the surroundings – the path begins to curve round to the left. A sharp zigzag affords me a brief view of something in the distance. The far-away sights and sounds of industry. What appear from way up here to be giant pipes laid out beside each other, careering down the hillside. Given their distance from where I stand the scale of the things must surely be immense. The large mass of nearby water kickstarts the grey cells' razorsharp powers of deduction into action and I conclude that I must be looking at some kind of water treatment plant. Elementary, my dear reader. The path then realigns itself with the natural curvature of the hillside and continues its descent.

This is a first-rate stretch of walking as the path clings to the side of the hill, its light stony form still in striking contrast to the dark mossy green of the landscape through which it runs. As though it had been burned across the vista – a white hot lightning bolt scorched into the black mountainous terrain. I can see rows of rooftops emerging through the far-away treetops and suddenly have the sense that the trail is, at least temporarily, transporting me from the wilderness back towards civilization. There are still a few miles ahead of me before I reach the comparative metropolis on the horizon – but the fact that I can actually now see the end of today's hike causes the muscles to begin whinging and moaning. The aged feet have been eerily well-behaved throughout this trip so far. Not a blister in sight and any aching has subsided within an hour-or-so of rest. They've woken up now though and are beginning to protest. The pressure points are suddenly grimacing with every step taken. The constant downhill of the last few miles undoubtedly hasn't helped in that regard – and looking ahead of me now it's clear that the situation is going to get worse before it gets better. It's pretty heroic stuff.

I reach a footbridge crossing over a jagged looking stream and take the opportunity to give the boots a quick rinse off. The poor old blighters are looking a touch forlorn it has to be said. Over the next few minutes, as the track continues to hang onto the hillside for dear life, the dramatic views ahead begin to disappear behind the hills that surround Kinlochleven. The views of the village itself and the surrounding area however, are opening up and becoming increasingly enticing, as the calf muscles begin to scream in harmony with the feet. Those pipes have re-appeared on the scene as well and have taken on something of a science fiction atmosphere as they aggressively envelop the landscape ahead. The trail then reaches the large area of woodland that it's been visibly heading towards for the last twenty minutes or so.

The thin stony track merges into a wider lane which, it's safe to assume, is used as an access road to the water treatment plant. Once under the cover of trees the first thing to strike me is that scores of people have once again appeared – as if from nowhere. The village is only a couple of miles away now and it seems as though a good number of its inhabitants have decided that a stroll in the shade of the woods is the ideal tonic to the heat of the July afternoon. In spite of my growing discomfort in the foot department I find myself agreeing with them wholeheartedly. The woods are a vibrant spectrum of greens, intensified by the sunlight that floods through every available breach in tree cover. The sedate and pleasant ambiance is so at odds with the wildness of the day, that the desolation of the moors and grandeur of the mountains all of a sudden seem as though they were a distant blurry dream.

The lane swirls back and forth flamboyantly as it continues to descend. After a short while I reach a rather snazzy-looking stone bridge, from which I can see the high uniform wall of a dam standing proud a few yards further up the stream. I'm beginning to drag my feet as I continue onwards and the path straightens out. I get more views of the giant pipes through the trees, but am struggling to maintain an interest now as my feet begin to throb. With alarming rapidity, the woods around me turn from a relaxing afternoon stroll in the shade to an endless and merciless torture. I'm moaning on a bit here, aren't I? Oh well, let's just say the woods drag on for ages and I'm really rather tired by this point. I probably pass several other points of interest that a better guide than myself would be able to relay to you with rapturous enthusiasm – but as I'm very busy feeling sorry for myself I don't notice any of them, which means you'll just have use your imagination. Trees, pipes, people, streams, et cetera.

After what feels like the passing of several decades, I finally emerge from the woods and arrive exhausted at the foot of a huge factory-type building. Several of the large pipes that I've been glimpsing frequently over the last hour or two come to an end here and seem to disappear into the building itself. There are crowds of people gathered enjoying the sunshine and I find a spot on the grass where I plonk myself down unceremoniously. I open up Mr B. and do some internet searching to learn what I can regards the treatment plant and its sci-fi piping system. It's named Blackwater Reservoir and is actually in place for the purpose of smelting aluminium. I don't really know what that means and so decide to look this up as well. (The amount of research and sheer hard-work that's gone into providing you with this informative and enthralling read is mind-boggling, dear reader.) It's the process of extracting aluminium from its oxide, of course – generally via the Hall process. As if it could be any other…! And what does any of that mean? Look, I don't know, OK? This is a hiking book. I did my best, had a good crack at the thing but, truth be told, as soon as I read the word 'metallurgical' the theme tune to Ski Sunday started playing in my head (which *is* interesting actually, because I didn't even realise I knew the theme tune to Ski Sunday) and I drifted off.

I'm brought back to reality by the sight of an elderly gent standing over me.

'You look tired,' he says, looking down at my somewhat sorry carcass. He has a kindly face with small rectangular spectacles perched on his nose and a thick crop of wavy white hair. He's thin, slightly stooped and dressed in a very sensible anorak with a dog lead drooped over his shoulders. I quickly deduce that this belongs to the muddy spaniel standing a few feet behind him.

The mutt has his back to us in a gesture that clearly states; 'I cannot believe we have stopped to talk to this idiot. I was promised a walk. Now can we please, for the love of all that is good, just get going again?'

'You been up the top today?' he says, glancing back up the path that leads through the woods to the mountains beyond.

'Yes, I'm walking the West Highland Way,' I say in reply. He smiles broadly down at me.

'Good for you, good for you. The spirit is willing but the legs can't cut the mustard these days I'm afraid... I expect it was a pretty picture up there today, was it?' he says leaning perilously over me in enthusiastic anticipation of my response.

I have sudden twin pangs of sympathy and empathy towards the fellow. I'm overcome by the notion that I'm speaking to my future self. What happens to the hiking obsessive when the leg muscles finally give up the ghost? I picture myself as an old man, spending my days hanging around national trust car parks at the bottom of hills throughout Somerset – holding a bag full of Kendall Mint Cake. 'Been up the top, have you?... Pretty was it, yes?... Pretty today I'd expect was it?... Got any pictures, have you?... Go on show me a picture, please just one picture... Look here, have some Kendal Mint Cake'. I shake off this horrific image and tell him that it was indeed very pretty up top today. We chat for several minutes about the trail in general and some experiences he's had walking it over the years. He also tells me that the dam I passed earlier was built by hand and that just beyond it lies the reservoir itself. The smelting factory (which he thankfully doesn't try and explain to me) is still used as a power station to provide electricity to the national grid.

I eventually clamber back to my feet and ask the chap if he's walking the same way as myself; into Kinlochleven.

'No, I'd better take this one into the woods for a bit or I'll never hear the end of it,' he says looking adoringly at the spaniel, who is still standing with its back to us. He wishes me luck for the rest of the trail and we depart.

The walk through Kinlochleven to the pub where I've booked a room for the night is a tad longer than expected. It takes me through a housing estate before veering off to spend a brief spell along a quaint riverside path. Once I emerge from the path and out into the centre of the village I'm struck by the size of the place. It feels more like a town than a village and is easily the largest inhabited area I've set foot in since leaving Milngavie on the first day of the trail. There are shops, cafés and even a museum. A main road runs through its centre and I walk on the pavement beside it in search of the pub. The village itself was originally built purely to house the workers of the smelting electricity sci-fi pipe factory (see previous page for detailed explanation) but has since grown into a thriving tourist destination. It was also – no doubt due to the aluminium water power dam thingy – the first village in the world to have every home connected to electricity.

Its size and main road mean it's not quite as attractive as most of the small isolated stopovers up to this point but - in the afternoon sunshine at the end of one of the most memorable and spectacular day's walking I've ever had – it's a dashed charming place to be strolling through. There are fellow ramblers all about the place, herds of tired aching limbs and smiling exhilarated faces. They shuffle along the pavements weighed down by backpacks and tents, they gather inside cafés in search of nourishment. Several of them sit sipping beverages on wooden benches that stand outside the (unbelievably welcome sight) of the pub. A simple nondescript affair that here and now looks to me like a magical palace of wonder. I pick my way through the discarded backpacks and cheerful revellers to the front entrance.

The simple and unpretentious exterior is matched inside with traditional décor throughout. Fluffy carpets, a fruit machine, tables and chairs and a well-stocked bar that gleams and sparkles enticingly. I order a pint of the heather ale and collapse onto a barstool. The bartender is a welcoming fellow with a tea towel slung over his shoulder in a manner that somehow adds the final flourish to the trusty old local pub ambiance.

'Good walk?'

'Yes, fantastic thanks.'

'How far you come? Kinghouse?'

'No, Bridge of Orchy.'

(Whistles) 'That's some walk, pal... You'll be needing this then,' he says as he hands me the aforementioned beverage. He's not wrong, dear reader. After I've swigged it down gratefully I check in and head up to my room.

I spend an hour or so cleaning myself up and resting the sorry old feet. Lying on the bed I listen (for the third time) to the audiobook version of the unreasonably excellent ghost story; *Dark Matter* by Michelle Paver. I always make sure I fill up the phone with audiobooks and music when embarking on a long-distance hike such as this. I never listen to anything whilst actually hiking you understand... For some reason that simply wouldn't do. But it does make the evenings pass by more easily for the solitary walker. For this particular trip I'm also accompanied by numerous PG Wodehouse (standard inclusion – never go anywhere without some Wodehouse to hand, you're bound to need one) as well as a few thrillers and a couple of Terry Pratchett for good measure. Musically I'm joined in the Scottish wilderness by, of course, Carter the Unstoppable Sex Machine... if you haven't cottoned on yet, they are the greatest band of all time. The latest Jim Bob album (ex-frontman of said greatest band of all time), the new Suede album, which is buttock-clenchingly excellent and the best of Chris TT, which is very much likewise. I appreciate you didn't ask... But I feel it important that you're able to build a full picture of your gallant narrator. So now you know – I'm very cool... *very cool*.

Later that evening I'm finishing off a plate of pizza and chips (the two great culinary behemoths reunited at last) and very much enjoying a second ale. The pub continues to bustle as the ramblers have now been joined by a smattering of locals. As with every establishment I've stopped in thus far there are a veritable plethora of different languages being spoken. Once the hearty meal is dispatched I have a brief conversation with a Spanish lady, who is also staying at the pub and walking the trail on her own. Over the course of the following half-an-hour or so, until she retires to her room, we chat and I discover that she's had an alarmingly eventful week. In fact – truth be told and cards on the table – if she were to write a book it would be a vastly more exciting tome than my own, dear reader. She arrived in Milngavie, from Spain, only to discover that the hotel had no record of her booking. After much arguing she ended up having to get a taxi to the nearest campsite (which - she wants on record – the hotel refused to pay for). She then caught some sort of virus and spent three days walking whilst being – and I received a really quite vivid and lengthy description of this – regularly ill, from more than one exit point. To finish matters off, earlier today she received an email from home advising her that the house which she shares with friends has been burgled.

'Well we've all suffered... I had to spend a whole night in a tent! My stringy cheeses have gone floppy and I've run out of Strawberry Weetabix drinks.' I don't actually say any of this of course. She has enough on her plate so it seems the gentlemanly thing to do is to bear the weight of my own burden

115

in stoical silence. Despite this tale of woe, she seems remarkably chipper and we go on to wax lyrical regards Rannoch Moor before she departs.

I then allow myself a moment or two of reflection as the reality dawns on me that tomorrow is the last stretch of the trail. 15 or so miles of rugged Highland beauty are now all that stands between me and Fort William. The enormity of this trail means that the previous few days seem both to have passed by in a flash and also to have lasted an eternity. The contrast between the day-to-day chatter of the locals, talking about the match being played on the large flat-screen TV that dominates one corner of the pub, and the various exotic languages in conversation all around me somehow echoes my feelings. The real world is slyly creeping its way unwanted into the grand adventure. Beginning to dilute the other-worldliness of the previous week with a potent dose of stinky old normality.

I always manage to work myself into this sombre frame of mind as the end of a trail looms into view. You needn't pay it any attention, dear reader. I fear it's really no more than the result of an over-analytical mind combined with a general lack of intelligence. I muster some resolve, give myself a stout talking to and then focus on the fact that I not only have another hike across this enchanting landscape to look forward to tomorrow, but there's also the small additional matter of climbing the UK's largest mountain the following day. Besides – it's Champions League. With spirits rejuvenated and thoughts of the incredible day I've just had still in my mind, I find a seat with a decent view of the screen and enjoy the match.

DAY SIX

Fort William

Kinlochleven

Day 6: Kinlochleven to Fort William

The Last Hurrah, Isn't that a Golden Eagle?
& Is this Ham Vegetarian?

I haven't even lifted the cursed eyelids the following morning and I'm already painfully aware that some contemptible blaggard has apparently crept into my room during the small hours and funnelled wet concrete into my cranium via the earhole... Either that or one too many ales were dispatched last night. The whining throb endured by the battle-hardened feet not eighteen hours prior, rather than retreating as previously assumed, has in fact simply relocated to a small area just behind my retina and resumed its foul symphony with odious fervour. This is treachery... By what or whom it matters not... I am wronged. Surely - as all of Scotland is my witness - I am wronged. No foul merciless misery of such concentration can plausibly be of mine own doing. Avenge me, dear reader, for it is treachery. 'Treachery!' I cry... Or rather silently wince.

After twenty minutes or so of mental preparation I finally stagger to my feet. I delicately feel my way to the bathroom, squinting and grimacing as all about me pulsates and throbs. I down 174 glasses of water and neck a couple of paracetamols. I then tentatively edge my way back to the bed and perch on the end of it for a further twenty minutes. Slowly the foul mists begin to recede and the world gradually starts to make some sort of sense again. I'm too old for this nonsense. It would appear that at some point during the previous evening my brain regressed by a few decades and was suddenly labouring under

119

the illusion that it was the mid-nineties and I was a virile young waif with the world at my feet. I am of course no such thing. This is 2017 and I am a middle-aged man on a walking holiday. I begin to pack my things and get ready for the off. I cast a fleeting look at the last remaining banana Weetabix drink. By way of a sudden reflux of fire and brimstone my belly sends me a clear message: 'Keep that thing away from me'. Fair enough – a sound supposition to which I duly adhere.

By the time I leave the pub and step out into the bright early morning sunshine my senses have returned. I'm invigorated and ready to embrace the day ahead. Well – I can see again and am dashed glad to be out in the fresh air at any rate. So this is it, dearest reader. The final day… One last hurrah. Your daring narrator must don the armour (muddy boots, smelly clothes and a really big bag) one last time and bravely forge a path to victory (follow a heavily waymarked trail to the pleasant town of Fort William) The odds were against me (no they weren't), they said it couldn't be done (who said what couldn't be done?), yet here I stand (that bit's true) on the cusp of an historic victory (near the end of a long walk). Brace yourselves; there will be drama, heartache and heroism. (Can't say for sure… But it seems unlikely.) There will be blood, sweat and tears. (There'll be sweat. Blood is unlikely… Maybe a nosebleed if I overdo it.) Join me for one last adventure… Oh, well apart from that really big mountain I'm climbing tomorrow of course… I really need to stop forgetting about that.

To kick off, the trail follows the road out of Kinlochleven as it turns left and heads towards the main body of water that makes up Loch Leven itself. I had supposed I'd be spending some time strolling along the banks of the loch this morning but a glance at the (increasingly tatty and dishevelled) pages of Mr B. informs me that this is as close as I'll get. I'm therefore slightly nonplussed and a smidge disappointed when I arrive at a waymarker pointing right, away from the loch and towards a path that heads off into the woods. A large old iron sign proclaiming 'Path to Fort William' provides an early reminder that I'm approaching the trail's end. The path then begins to climb at an increasingly steep gradient. Initially this perturbs your narrator a touch, I'm sorry to report. 'Great... I expected a gentle amble along the loch in the sunshine to caress the hangover from the remorseful old system and instead I'm climbing uphill through more woods.' As has already been established beyond doubt; S. Reynolds is an optimistic, glass half full sort of chap... So I'm as shocked as you to discover this dour display of negative sentiment, dear reader. Fortunately – as is so often the case – the trail knows best. The woods are full of attractive birch trees and a short uphill slog, away from the glare of the sun, is exactly what the doctor ordered - vis-à-vis the foresaid delicate condition.

That being said, as time moves on it becomes apparent that this particular uphill slog was not to be all that short. I'm working up a sweat as the climb continues via some stone steps and cobbled paths. The Albatross is weighing heavy and the ankles have decided that now is the ideal moment to resume itching with a quite unnecessary and downright unsportsmanlike intensity. I spend a few minutes walking backwards so as to give one set of leg muscles a rest and let another set take the strain. I think this is pretty dashed street smart of me all things considered - and am busy heaping some hard-earned praise upon the inspired grey cells when I lose my footing spectacularly and fall on my backside with a bruising thump. Or to be more accurate I fall on The Albatross with a bruising thump and then struggle to get to my feet for an embarrassing length of time... Think of an overturned woodlouse and you've got the gist of the thing.

After spending a few moments massaging the ego as well as the backside, I continue the climb. I reach a clearing in the trees and an arresting view of the loch and Kinlochleven opens up below me and stops me in my tracks. The trail certainly does know best. Today is the clearest I've experienced thus far and it's as though the season has changed overnight. It's almost a new landscape as the dark atmospheric Highland fury has subsided and been replaced by the brilliant vibrancy of summer. The loch shimmers a rich deep blue that mirrors the cloudless sky above. The village and the mountainous terrain beyond it blur through a filter of heat haze. I move onwards and upwards as the Avon SSS melts away. I travel through more smattering's of tree cover providing me with temporary shelter from the glower of the sun.

In between the woodland stretches, clearings in the trees provide increasingly awesome reimaginings of the same view of the landscape and the village behind me. The higher I get the more I see and the greater the sense of scale. I've been overwhelmed by the grandeur and scale of this landscape at every turn, yet seeing it now in these crystal-clear conditions somehow manages to heighten this perspective even further still. Winding tracks criss-cross the trails path as I ascend – each one seems to beckon me with the promise of adventures new. The trail itself continues its straight and true course upwards however, and with every step I take the overindulgences of the previous evening are falling away.

I've hit the early sweet-spot of the hike. Again, I've no idea if this is peculiar to yours truly or something that all we in the rambling community experience. We brothers and sis... Actually no, I'd scrapped the sibling thing, hadn't I? We kindred spirits united by the noble... Actually, I'll just get on with it. Usually somewhere between one and two hours into the hike I hit this, almost euphoric, sweet-spot. For all I know it may be a biological thing; endorphins releasing after a certain amount of exertion or whatnot (my medical knowledge being at a similar level to my knowledge of geology, insects and trees). Whatever the reason, I have a half-hour spell of jubilant joy and wonder. An idiotic smile plastered across the face and a bouncing spring in the step. That truly wondrous knowledge that there is quite literally nothing on this earth that you want other than to be right here, right now. A pure and untainted contentment that only the trail can provide.

My high spirits are maintained as I reach the summit of the 'short uphill slog'. Amongst the mountains that gloriously fill the distant horizon I spy a distinctive triangular peak. It looks like a cartoon mountain that someone's superimposed onto the backdrop. I consult Mr B. to be advised that it's the Pap of Glencoe. 'What's a Pap, Mr B.?' I enquire, having reached the stage of isolation where I'm no longer able to keep my insane dialogue with inanimate objects safely concealed within my own head. Mr B. remains tight-lipped and so I instead look ahead along the trail at what awaits me. The path picks up another of those old disused military roads and heads off across a pleasingly flat landscape. Or rather, to be more accurate, the path sets off along a striking glen with vast hillsides on either side – so the terrain around the path itself is flat but all about me is anything but.

It's difficult to believe I'll be in Fort William and the end of the trail within mere hours, as I look out across the majestic vista. The final day of a trail can, on occasion, be as lacklustre as the opening day. The need to bring the walker back to a centre of civilization from which they can reasonably expect to travel homewards being the reality that necessitates this. It's with a sense of genuine gratitude and respect for this incredible trail therefore that I march onwards through a stretch of Highlands as dramatic and remote as any I've walked through over the last six days. There are similarities to Rannoch Moor in the desolate beauty of the scene. The feeling of being in an unchanged ancient world almost untouched by humanity. Yet it's also markedly different to Rannoch in ways I'm unsure I can adequately convey.

'Great...' I hear you cry.

'Perhaps you could have a stab at it S. Reynolds, old thing? Given that you're looking at it and we're, you know... not.'

OK, dear reader, I'll have a pop at it and see what happens. It's browner. How's that? Alright, alright... It may just be the weather, I suppose. The storm clouds and driving wind and rain were integral to my experience on Rannoch Moor. The bright sunshine of this clear July morning transforms the land into something more arid. I mean it's not arid obviously... There are reflective mountain streams strewn about the place and whatnot. But its character is somehow parched – as equally desolate and dramatic as yesterday's stretch but in a different way. That's as good as you're going to get I'm afraid.

As I make my way onwards I'm continuing to cross over the numerous foresaid reflective streams. They provide a strange moving element to the otherwise motionless panorama, as they flow steadily down the hillsides like cracks in broken glass. I pass a few isolated windswept trees standing lonely and battered in the emptiness. These too take on a different guise in the clement conditions. The absence of any wind means that rather than appearing to be the battle-hardened warriors, the last men standing, like their counterparts on Rannoch Moor, they're instead almost comical. As though they're striking an exaggerated pose, or were pulling a silly face when the wind changed direction and now they're stuck that way forever. These thoughts make me feel a bit guilty and I affectionately pat a branch or two on my way past; 'Sorry, old thing'.

A short while later I pass through a decidedly eerie area strewn with abandoned and rusting old farm machinery. The ruins of a building, presumably an old farmhouse, sit a little way back from the path. This initially brings to mind post-apocalyptic books and movies like The Stand or The Road - as though some catastrophic natural disaster stopped life dead decades ago and I'm the first human being to set foot here since then. As I walk through the once inhabited farmland however I'm hit by a quieter and more real sense or sorrow. People lived their lives on this patch of wilderness. They laughed and cried here, harboured their hopes and dreams here. They worked tirelessly at a way of life long since forgotten. They understood this wild and magical land in ways that those of us passing through never will. As with the ghostly bothies and ruins that I've already passed on this trip, something of the sweat and toil of this farmsteads long since departed inhabitants still lingers. Some faint impression carried on the breeze that permeates the rusting carcasses and crumbling rubble.

It would doubtless be enough to spook a lesser soul and even your fearless narrator feels the faint flutter of the old heebie-jeebies from deep within. A second set of isolated ruins a few minutes further along the path does little to quell the sensation. Once past this ethereal enclave however, I'm again left to bask in the grandeur of my surroundings. If something of the jagged edge of the place is missing in these picturesque weather conditions, the sheer scale of things is as astonishing as ever. That sensation of timelessness is still there as well. All the centuries of human endeavour at once seem so fragile and insignificant – an unremarkable aside that has left its scars but is ultimately forgotten.

I pass over more streams and fords as the path meanders gently onwards. I'm singing the words to *You Can't Take It With You* by the mighty Jim Bob out loud as I plod along. The volume of this outburst increases to a level that I wouldn't usually brave unless behind closed doors. *'You can't take it with you, where you're going - You won't need a bus fare if the wind is blowing – We'll sing a song for you and read a poem'.* I stop still and hold my hands triumphantly aloft; *'Everything will be the way you want to leave it – The meaning of your life will stay a secret – I cross my heart and hope that I can keep it too'*. I'm now positively bellowing it out across the empty Highlands; *'We'll get some flowers and we'll drive them round – At five miles an hour to the other side of town – We'll re-arrange them on some sacred ground'*... I then spy a couple of chaps on the path up ahead and am promptly awakened from my virtuoso solo performance. They're still some way off – it's not really possible to catch someone by surprise in this landscape – nevertheless noise travels. I was giving it some welly so to speak. Then there's the Freddie Mercury pose I was striking with arms raised and legs apart. Let's just say the three-minute walk towards them until we eventually pass each other is an awkward one for yours truly. They make no comment over and above the cordial good mornings and nice-day-for-its, although I do possibly detect a desire not to linger near the strange singing man with shiny skin as they abruptly stride off into the distance.

Eventually the path begins to turn to the right and climb slightly. A large area of woodland becomes visible up ahead. Mr B. pipes up to advise me that I'll soon be passing some old shielings. 'What are shielings, Mr B.?' I say, before checking myself again. It's only been a week and I appear to have gone completely doolally. This behaviour needs to be reined in, Reynolds, you'll be back in the hue and cry of civilization soon. Do I mean hue and cry? I feel like I've said hue and cry a few times in this book already... What is hue and cry anyway? Weren't they a band from the eighties? Doesn't matter, the point is I need to get used to pretending I'm normal again and quicksharp. I read on to discover that shielings are a type of makeshift house used in centuries gone by to provide shelter to shepherds tending their flocks during the summer months.

As well as the remains of these old stone structures the path passes through a series of similarly striking sheepfolds on its way towards the looming woods. The path has flattened out and the going is easy as the trail is gobbled up by the forest once again. I'm not plunged into the darkness on this occasion however as the trees part to leave room for the wide and rocky dirt track on which I now stroll. This feeling of continued openness despite the surrounding woodland gives this stretch of a walking a new character, unlike anything else on the trail thus far. It also perfectly suits the sunny day as the vivid green of the pine forest, previously so dark and shadowy, now emanates a rich warmth that temporarily keeps any notions of the pending trail's end locked away behind a carefree veneer. The tree-cover breaks completely at regular intervals to reveal brief glimpses of the views beyond.

After another twenty minutes or so I come to a larger clearing where the track divides. An enticing bench sits overlooking a hypnotic view of Lochan Lunn Da-Bhra and the surrounding moorland. I take some time to soak it up, increasingly conscious of the fact that I'm running out of breath-taking Highland panoramas with every moment that passes. A buzzard circles in the distance, with its distinctive v-shaped wingspan silhouetted against the sky. I follow its progress, utterly mesmerised, for a good few minutes more before finally getting going again. The track I've been following veers off to the left to merge with something more akin to a country road – whilst the West Highland Way turns right and back into the forest.

This shorter spell of woodland walking brings with it an almost deftly silence. The only sounds are those of my boots on the now thin single file track underfoot and the faintest suggestion of running water off to my left. This has continued to be a trail full of contrasts; the empty landscape full of wildlife, the dark and the light, the beauty and the bloodshed. I've never been on a trail so full of fellow ramblers, yet there have been many moments of complete isolation such as this one – where I feel that there can't possibility be another soul for miles in any direction. As if to provide confirmation of its gloriously volatile character the trail then abruptly leaves the woodland behind and I find myself out in the open, climbing a hill in the bright sunshine. After a few sweaty minutes of ascent, I reach the summit and another view of the lochan below.

I decide that this is the ideal place for a spot of luncheon. As you've no doubt gathered by now this, in reality, means a couple of Mars Bars and some warm water. As I look out across the wild views I set the old grey cells to the task of devising a viable long-term alternative lunch menu, for hikes such as this. Stringy cheese snacks – as undeniably scrumptious as they are – have proved insufficient and not as long lasting as one would perhaps assume. I've previously experimented with other cheese related products with similarly below-par results. With actual bona fide honest-to goodness cheese from an actual real-life cow of the four-legged and mooing variety (which since going vegetarian makes up somewhere in the region of 85% of my normal diet away from the trail – the other 15% being mainly Mars Bars) you have the same issue regards longevity... Everything gets a bit sweaty and smelly around day four – and so does the cheese. (Boom! Thanks very much, plenty more where that came from.)

I could always start carrying a stove I suppose. Then again, my instinct has told me since day one of discovering a passion for hiking that this would be a bad idea. I'm liable to, at best, give myself food poisoning and, at worst, set fire to myself and a large area of surrounding countryside. I can - maybe - find a way to maintain my heroic adventurer reputation through the whole camping scandal (or 'Tent-gate', as I'm now calling it), but I think that becoming known as the rambler who set fire to an ancient forest whilst trying to cook a boil-in-the-bag vegetable biryani might just prove to be a bridge too far in that regard. As a general rule my instinct is a trifle lacking. Notably absent during many scenarios wherein an on-the-ball instinct should be looking to take charge and earn its daily crust and so forth. It seems prudent therefore, on the rare occasions when the fellow does deem the situation worthy of his presence, to yield obediently and give the thing no further thought. All of which means that the old grey cells are well and truly stumped. No sense dwelling on the thing, the Mars Bars are... Well, everyone likes Mars Bars, don't they? I wonder what *would* happen if I only ate Mars Bars forevermore... There's a book in that, dear reader.

Afternoon

After rinsing down the last of the caramel and nougat exquisiteness with a swig of the old lukewarm, I don the pack and carry on. The path clings to the side of the hill in the manner that so many of the best paths invariably tend to do. The views continue to be fantastic and yours truly is full of vim and vigour re the afternoon ahead. I'm walking towards another cluster of woodland when, as the path undulates and reaches another mini-summit, the awesome sight of Ben Nevis comes into focus through the heat haze above the treeline. The path is heading straight towards the mighty old mountain and the climax of the whole week now proudly dominates the vista. It's enough to make the old heart strut its stuff with gay abandon, dear reader. My eyes are fixed on the famous summit as the path winds its way back into the forest.

A few minutes later I reach a wooden bridge that crosses over a fast-flowing stream as it carves its way through the dense woodland. The woods then part once again and the track widens so that the scene resembles that of earlier this morning. Ben Nevis re-appears directly up ahead through the gap in the trees and I'm again staring up at it slack-jawed as I stride onwards. This situation is maintained for some time and for a while, as the mountain appears to get no closer at all, I feel as though time may have stopped. Were that the case, there are far worse places in which to spend eternity. Although I would perhaps feel as though I were trapped in a clichéd metaphor for life. Forever striding toward, but never actually reaching, the end goal. All hard work and no progress. Soon enough though the scene does change as I reach another footbridge. This one leads me briefly out into the open for no more than few yards before plunging me straight back into more forest.

From here on in the going gets a good deal tougher. The trail has a sting in its tail, as though it were reacting to my clever trapped in a time-loop observation. (see previous paragraph – or just remember it... I mean you've only just read it after all.) 'So you think it's all getting a bit samey do you, Reynolds? Well how about,,, this!?' The path drops away suddenly and I'm now negotiating a steep and tricky descent into the depths of the woods. Somewhere approximately two thirds of the way down a series of (slightly precarious-looking) steps are carved into the hillside to guide the walker to the forest floor. When I get there, I'm greeted by a pleasingly overgrown jungle-like scene full of jagged mossy rocks and contrasting shades of green and orange. The loud and exotic squawk of a bird from somewhere way up above adds a timely flourish to complete the picture. I mean to say, it's almost certainly a crow – but still.

Another footbridge crosses over an enthusiastic babbling stream that seems as though it's in a hurry to be somewhere. The path then immediately sets about climbing up the other side of the valley, with an ascent that – at the very least – is a match for the descent I've just completed. It's not long before I'm letting out an undignified pant as I continue to climb. I squint my eyes in reaction to the now all too familiar sting of

Avon Skin So Soft, as it mingles with a fresh layer of sweat. I'm buzzing though. The trail has again thrown up something new and the perspiration feels like confirmation of its stubborn refusal to go quietly. Burn out don't fade away. The climb relaxes slightly and begins to plateau – the path itself does not however, and instead begins to wind and undulate with an erratic beauty.

The stony dirt track darts around as if it were an overexcited child. Fleeting glimpses of the mountainous horizon are revealed and then removed with each writhing turn. Although no longer steep, I am still climbing and I feel the muscles in my legs begin to grumble. I ignore their protests heroically however and indeed am not too far off skipping along, as the path continues to weave its course. I pass by a few other tracks that veer off from the trail in all directions before eventually coming to a large fence. Here another track winds off to the right and a sign advises me that it's this way for the Dun Deardail hillfort. Mr B. chips in and explains that this is a recent addition to the trail and provides a brief and worthwhile detour to see the remains of the ancient hillfort. I'm enjoying myself immensely however and am on the brink of ignoring Mr B.'s suggestion and carrying on along the main path. In the end though – and in the spirit of growth and maturity that has defined this noble quest thus far – I decide to go the extra mile.

To say this was the correct decision is something of an understatement. The short walk takes me from the woods out into a clearing where the remains of the fortification lie. The views are utterly spectacular. The fort stands overlooking the forests below. Ben Nevis rears up in all its grandiose ferocity. I also get my first sight of Fort William in the far distance. The immediate landscape surrounding the hillfort is straight from the pages of *Lord of the Rings*; a velvet green blanket draped over the jagged hillside. Mr B. advises me that Dun Deardail is a vitrified fort. Basically, dearest reader old thing, this means that at some point in its history the fort has been on fire. It could have been during a battle or some kind of natural event. Whatever the reasons the remains show all the tell-tale signs of exposure to extreme heat.

The full explanation may have been slightly more complicated and indeed comprehensive. It's difficult to be certain, you understand, because as soon as I began reading about silicate materials the theme tune to Question of Sport kicked in again. There's definitely a geological and/or archaeological trigger to that particular theme tune. I should start writing this down. Anyway, the point being that the thing has been ruddy hot at some point. It's an incredible spot and most certainly worth the short detour. Not all such remains of forts and whatnots are guaranteed to be worth your while, I've found. As a walker you do come across a number of them on your travels. Frightfully interesting from an historical perspective of course. But in terms of the spectacle I've often found that I might very well have walked straight past the things without noticing them, were I not pre-advised of their presence. Not in this case however. The prominent and dramatic location mean that it's all too easy to visualise just how incredible this particular ancestral stronghold would once have been.

After walking back and rejoining the trail proper the path leads me into Nevis Forest. The character of this chameleon of a trail once again changes in a heartbeat. The winding twitchy path of earlier is replaced by a languid sprawling track that nonchalantly begins what will surely be the final descent into Fort William. I'm now essentially circumnavigating one side of Ben Nevis. A valley, through which the road leading into the town and the River Nevis run in tandem, separates me from the foot of the mountain. Nevis Forest – like the path itself – is spread out lazily in either direction. It's far less dense than any other woodland I've walked through today and large bare patches of the hillsides are visible through the gaps in the trees.

The sun's heat is intensifying as the afternoon stretches on and the cornflower blue sky is clearer than I've seen it all week. For the first time in hours there are people within view. I can see numerous moving dots on the landscape up ahead; another telltale sign that I'm close to the journey's end. The first pair I pass are a couple of chaps, probably about my age, who stop me for a quick chinwag.

'What a day for it, eh? Are you just completing the whole trail?' One of them cheerfully enquires; a tall fellow with such a generous layer of sun cream plastered over his face that it looks as though the Chuckle Brothers must have just splatted him with one of their custard pies.

'Yes, that's right. Apart from that old thing tomorrow of course,' I reply, gesturing towards Ben Nevis. 'What about you guys?'

'A group of us walked it last year but us two had to leave before we got to climb Ben Nevis... So we've come back to put that right.'

'Oh, good stuff,' I say – resisting the temptation to launch into my *doing the West Highland Way and not climbing Ben Nevis is like...* spiel.

We chat for a few minutes more and I discover that they're also climbing the mountain tomorrow and so I promise to keep an eye out for them. I pass a few more folks over the next half-a-mile or so until the trail abruptly turns right. A steep descent follows that leads me past a graveyard and eventually emerges from the woodland for the final time. A track then leads down to the road, where the path picks up the pavement. I glance at good old Mr B. only to have my suspicions confirmed; that that's pretty much it. The trail will now follow the road all the way into Fort William. Not a fantastic last couple of miles I grant you, but the day as a whole has been a worthy conclusion to this incredible trail.

A mile or so later I pass a giant boulder a few yards back from the side of the road. A small middle-aged woman in a leather waistcoat and top hat is hopping in circles around it, laughing hysterically. A man, presumably her partner, is clapping along delightedly as she goes. It transpires that this is the famous Samuel's Stone. A wishing stone that has a number of elaborate legends attached to it. It is said that you must hop around the stone three times and make a wish. If the stone moves (which it's apparently apt to do from time to time) then your wish will come true. I stand with the couple for a few minutes but, alas, the stone is resolute in its stillness. They try to encourage me to have a stab at it, but I suddenly feel a touch self-conscious and politely decline.

Fort William is a larger town than any other on this trail and is bustling with the sights and sounds of urban life when I arrive. I make my way through the comparative chaos towards the trail's end. It's pleasing to note that a large percentage of the crowds adorning the streets and roadsides are fellow ramblers, a few of them looking as shell-shocked by their surroundings as I feel. It's far from an unpleasant town in truth. Nestling as it does on the shores of Loch Linnhe with the majestic spectre of Ben Nevis ever-looming. The town centre is relatively nondescript, with your standard ensemble of high street chains all present and correct. It has kept some of its highland character however and, perhaps in part due to the continued popularity of this trail, still seems to celebrate rather than ignore its enviable setting.

When I eventually arrive at the statue marking the end of the trail the first thing I notice is that it proudly states: 'The original end of the West Highland Way'. After some investigation I discover that there are in fact two endings to the West Highland Way. This one - a large colourful number in the

134

shape of the iconic Scottish thistle – and a second, which is located further into the town centre. Ours is not to reason why and all that. I snap a few clumsy selfies and carry on towards the second finish line. This turns out to be an impressive statue of a chap sitting on a bench, with a map and sign standing behind him advising that *this* is, in fact, the end of the trail. This is the newer official ending and, truth be told, it makes sense. The previous one had a backdrop of a traffic jam and was something of an anti-climax. Here you have the view of Loch Linnhe and the mountains beyond. I take a few more obligatory selfies and sit for a while basking in my triumph.

I then check the phone to see exactly where my hotel for the night is located. Three miles outside of Fort William. That would be mistake number... Um... What are we up to? It's at moments like this that the resilient Reynolds spirit really comes into its own, dear reader. The sun is shining; the ambiance is one of summery serenity. Does S. Reynolds lament, under such conditions, the news of a few additional steps at the end of a bracing stroll? Grylls might... Mears almost certainly would... Bradbury would be calling a taxi as we speak. Not I, old thing, not I. It's with a cheerful gusto that I drape The Albatross over the shoulders and head off once more. The hotel is situated on a main road (my old friend the A82) outside of the town and the journey there consists of a saunter along the roadside pavement. There are worse pavements to be sauntering along however; Loch Linnhe keeps me company as it sparkles brilliantly in the afternoon light. A mile or so from the hotel I pass a father and son sat eating sandwiches on the bank of the river.

'Is that a golden eagle Daddy?'

I swirl round so quickly that the weight of the pack nearly causes me to lose my balance and tumble to the ground for the second time today.

'No, that's a pigeon Jack.'

Well there you have it... With that I finally let go of my dream of seeing the mighty eagle in flight. It would've been the icing on the cake; the turnip on the pizza if you will. That being said this trail has exceeded the expectations in every other regard and to grumble would be nothing short of churlish at this juncture. Besides – one of the many lessons garnered from time on the trail is that there is no such thing as disappointment or mundanity as far as old Mother Nature goes. A pigeon it maybe, but a pigeon is a beautiful thing. Especially a pigeon that's gliding effortlessly on the breeze over Loch Linnhe in the afternoon sunshine. I see many more folks contentedly adorning the riverbank as I continue on my way, basking in the warmth of the sun's rays. On the other side of the road I'm passing the detached properties of the well-to-do, with sprawling driveways and large windows and balconies that overlook the river. I mentally add the location to the ever-growing list of potential places to live once I become a world-famous author and national treasure. I'll probably have a little bolthole or two somewhere along most of the truly world class trails. I expect they'll end up becoming sites of pilgrimage for future generations of ramblers.

The sight of my hotel up ahead wrenches me from my imaginings. It does stand out rather amongst the plush houses and manicured lawns. It's more of a motel really, I assume built here by mistake just like the ski resort I passed yesterday. It would be more at home on a highway on the outskirts of a deserted town in the USA... Sometime in the late seventies. But not the real USA, the movie version... Starring a young Jack Nicholson on a moody cinematic road trip full of desolation and stark commentary on the human condition... That kind of thing. All it's missing is a giant neon sign with the word '_OTEL' flickering eternally in bright pink capital letters. The paintwork is peeling, the tarmac driveway is cracked, the... 'Alright, Reynolds, you pompous old bore, you're meant to be camping as I recall; how's that working out for you?' Fair point, dear reader, well made. Plus if it weren't for all of the aforementioned then the establishment would doubtless be well out of my increasingly meagre price range – as I'm afraid that the whole Tent-gate saga has meant that I've overspent to an almost catastrophic degree. Nothing ventured and all that. Once inside the place is perfectly pleasant, if still distinctly seventies in its general atmosphere. Faux wood panels throughout, and a curious abundance of green felt-covered noticeboards hanging all about the place. Most of which are empty save for hundreds of tiny multi-coloured drawing pins gathered in each corner. The friendly lady at reception, dressed in a uniform that surely started out in life belonging to a flight attendant, advises me that I must fill out my dinner menu choices before receiving the keys to my room. I consider this a little unconventional but, in the plucky spirit you'll have by now come to expect from me, I gamely oblige – ticking the vegetarian options without really paying attention.

On my way through the maze of corridors in search of my elusive room I pass several other hotel guests. I note that none of them are fellow ramblers. This should not be a surprise of course, as my sorrowful lack of brain power has left me miles from the trail in a hotel situated on a main road. It is nonetheless a trifle peculiar though. I stick out somewhat amongst the holidaying families and couples of advanced years (of which there seem to be many). The absence of muddy boots and oversized backpacks leaves me with the overwhelming sensation of being in the wrong place. Which of course is more or less the extent of it.

Once in my room I spend an hour or so having a wash and writing up some notes. I briefly consider that the additional few miles it took to reach the hotel will doubtless be a tad more of a nuisance tomorrow morning, when they'll precede a brisk stroll up the largest mountain in the UK. You'll be pleased to hear that I don't let this burden the soul however and instead head off to the dining hall in tiptop spirits. The clientele assembled in the large featureless hall reinforce the notion that I'm the only rambler on the guestlist. Coachloads of holidaymakers chat cheerfully and make toasts whilst hordes of, seemingly ownerless, children run about the place excitedly. I'm shown to my table by a girl who, like the lady at reception, appears to be dressed as a flight attendant. My table sits looking sorry for itself in the corner of the room. The only single-chaired table in the place, positioned to look disapprovingly out of the window with its back to the ongoing merriment.

I'm staring out of foresaid window and daydreaming when my starter arrives in the form of a bowl of soup. I thank the waitress, pick up the spoon and generally get set to plunge in, as is apt in these scenarios. It's pea and ham soup. There's no two ways about it... S. Reynolds might not be a culinary whizz per se, but I flatter myself that I know a bowl of pea and ham soup when it's presented to me. After a few failed clumsy attempts, I manage to catch the waitress's attention.

'Um... Is this ham vegetarian at all?'

(Pause) She looks at me in... well, in the manner you probably would look at someone who has just asked you that question.

'No... Sir... It isn't.'

'Ah... I'm, um... I'm vegetarian you see.'

After a few more awkwardly exchanged words she makes a call and a second waitress dressed as a flight attendant appears. She's carrying a copy of the menu choices form that I filled in at reception – which, and this will shock you, confirms beyond any doubt that I had indeed ticked the pea and ham soup option. The remaining two courses pass by without any further drama I'm pleased to report. A creamy spaghetti thingy followed by a slice of cake.

After successfully dispatching two of the three courses in my three-course meal (not a terrible success rate when you think about it, I suppose), I go for a brief stroll along the loch before returning to the hotel to prop up the bar for an hour or so. Whilst sipping on a whisky I call Tasha and we chat for twenty minutes or thereabouts, bringing each other up to speed regards our respective days. She informs me that our ageing house rabbit Bovril has disgraced himself once again by chewing her slippers to the extent that they have been rendered unusable. This makes me laugh raucously and my heart swells with love for the both of them. It's in this contented frame of mind that I eventually retire to my room, with mountains on my mind. Or rather one in particular.

DAY SEVEN

Ben Nevis

Day 7: The Summit

If you're the sort of fellow who gets so excited at the prospect of a day's hiking that you invariably wake up before the sun rises and can't then get back to sleep (I'm sure that there must be a few of you of out there), then it stands to reason that a pending jaunt up a mountain will only augment this defect further. One time insomniac plus excitement equals: hello, 4am. Furthermore, one time insomniac plus excitement plus bladder the size of a dried lentil equals... Well, it equals the same thing as it happens, but you grasp the essence of the thing I'm sure. I fill the additional time by drinking three cups of instant coffee and ceremoniously supping the last Weetabix drink of the trip. Not really a banana type of day, truth be told, but needs must. I then lather on the Avon SSS like war paint and don the armour for one last hurrah (again).

I haul The Albatross through the hotel, getting lost seven or eight times in the process, before finally finding the reception area and main exit. Outside the sun is obscured by cloud and the temperature (accepting that it's still an unearthly hour) is definitely a setting or two lower down on God's own thermostat, versus the previous day. In part this is no bad thing as today's walk is of course exclusively upward in nature. Although I do find myself suddenly contemplating the somewhat disheartening prospect of climbing Ben Nevis under a thick cover of cloud, thus not seeing a single thing besides the five feet of mountain directly in front of me. A slightly ironic end to the trail given the amazing views that have characterised the previous one hundred or so miles of walking.

You ought to know your intrepid narrator well enough by now though, dear reader. If you don't know me by now then consult Mick Hucknall for further details. (Wait... Did I just make a Simply Red gag?) As you'd therefore expect, this thought deters me not a single jot. (The cloud thing I mean... Not the Simply Red gag.) It's with nothing short of pluck and purpose that I put one foot in front of the other in the age-old manner of the noble rambler.

That being understood; foresaid pluck and aforementioned purpose are put to the test early on as the reality dawns that I'm, of course, still some four-or-so miles from the foot of the mountain. I must first traverse the roadside back into Fort William, then traverse the other roadside back out of Fort William. These things are sent to test us and all that... What doesn't kill you only makes you... tired before you've even got started? The few miles back into Fort William are far from wasted however. Somewhere a mile-or-so in the old grey matter wakes from its slumber to greet the day with dashed impressive results. I hatch a fiendishly cunning plan wherein I swing by the hotel I'm booked into tonight and ask to drop off The Albatross. Meaning I can climb the mountain sans cargo. Not just a pair of legs and an increasingly impressive moustache, dear reader! (Is it too late on in the proceedings to mention that I've grown a moustache?)

As fate would have it the hotel I'm booked into is a Premier Inn, so in one sense I'm back where I started from in Milngavie a week ago. When I eventually arrive the accommodating lady at reception is only too happy to... Um... Well - accommodate me – re my luggage drop-off request. When it comes down to it however, I find to my surprise that I can't quite bring myself to leave the old thing behind. We've gone this far together after all - and it suddenly seems a touch unappreciative to dump my overweight companion in a Premier Inn broom cupboard and go swanning off on my own. It turns out that I have no such sentimental concerns regards my tent, sleeping bag or roll mat however, and all three are joyfully discarded. As is the toiletry bag, change of shoes and the eye-wateringly funky bag of dirty laundry. I convey my gratitude and continue on my way carrying a large, more than half empty, backpack which now contains Mars Bars, water bottles, a phone charger and – of course – Mr B. I'm assuming his services won't really be required today. 'Keep going up' would seem to cover the instructions for the day's excursion. But as with The Albatross I find that I simply can't leave the old chap behind; doesn't seem proper somehow. I have - I believe - already mentioned that I've apparently gone completely doolally?

The following few miles back out of Fort William are pleasant enough and make a decent fist of maintaining my excitement regards the day ahead. The sun is now peeking tentatively through the clouds and the morning has an invigoratingly fresh and crisp feeling to it. The birds are singing cheerily in the trees adorning the roadside path and all is right with the world. Scores of fellow ramblers pepper the pavements and pathways – all heading, bleary-eyed, towards the mountain. As bizarre as it now seems I hadn't considered that anyone else would be climbing the thing at the same time as myself. In my daydreams I'd had the mountain to myself, save for the odd passing golden eagle or snow leopard. Absurd really – given the endless conga line of hikers I joined to climb Ben Lomond. It's now abundantly clear that this number will be at least tenfold greater on this occasion and that I'll be one of hundreds of people to complete the task today alone.

After a further twenty minutes or thereabouts, I arrive at the Ben Nevis visitor centre which marks the start of the climb. The place is heaving with hikers preparing for the off. The crowd ranges from serious-faced professionals in full body mountaineering get up; complete with poles, safety harnesses, mirrored skiing goggles and laminated maps – to families wearing jeans and trainers, looking all about them with concerned expressions on their faces that suggest that they may have slightly underestimated the nature of the day's outing. I pass a group of a dozen-or-so folks in matching bright yellow t-shirts sporting a charities logo. They're being given a lecture by their instructor regards the challenge ahead – including what to do if they should become stranded and need to be rescued. I sit down for a few minutes to mentally prepare myself for the off, next to a large chap with shoulder-length hair wearing a tight-fitting Metallica t-shirt and swigging on a can of cola. The whole scene is one of near comical contrasts that leaves me completely nonplussed regards what awaits.

After steeling myself and drawing from the sizeable Reynolds reserves of resolve I head heroically towards the starting point. I cross a space-age bridge over the River Nevis that could not be further from the numerous ancient stone arches and rickety wooden footbridges encountered throughout the hike. It's pretty cool though. A path then leads me along the riverside for a few hundred yards before veering left and uphill. I clamber over a stile as the track turns right again and spreads out across the hillside. As earlier deduced I'm part of an endless line of walkers disappearing off into the distance. If viewing the scene from far above it must resemble an anthill as we all scurry along in one busy procession. As the path continues to cut across the hillside it merges with other tracks rolling in from the right. First the original starting point in line with the Ben Nevis Inn (a pub seems a better start and end point to a mountain trail than a visitor centre if you ask me… Which, typically, nobody did of course), and then the trail leading up from the Glen Nevis Youth Hostel. I note that a few people around me are already needing to stop for a rest and I begin understand that what awaits us all will be no more or less than a gruelling war of attrition. Sometime later the path turns sharply to begin the ascent proper.

144

The views are beginning to open up as the path becomes a rocky stairway underfoot. It's carved from large boulders and for some reason I'm reminded of the old cartoon The Flintstones... Which then puts the theme tune to the old cartoon The Flintstones into my head... Where it remains, continually playing on a loop... For a very long time. At some point – whilst Fred Flintstone is banging on his front door and yelling at Wilma to let him in for about the four hundredth time – a thin elderly man runs past me. He must surely be in his late seventies at the very least and is wearing Lycra cycling shorts and a pair of those sunglasses that wrap around your head. He politely cries out 'Excuse me!' when anyone blocks his way as he continues to run up the path. He's also wearing a smile on his face that clearly says, 'That's right, you're seeing it... Highest mountain in the UK? No problem, what are we doing *after* breakfast?'

After what seems like a jolly long time I arrive at a footbridge crossing a mountain stream. A group of twenty-somethings stand to the side of the bridge debating whether or not to call it a day. I pause for a minute and let some faster climbers past before carrying on. The slog is relentless but, although the clouds are setting in now, the views of the vast valley below are more than adequate payoff for my efforts. The mountains off to the right are as dark and moody as they are gargantuan. Clouds obscure their peaks whilst hundreds of feet below the treetops already look like pinpricks. Far away roads and pathways are battle scars upon the skin of the ancient and weathered landscape. A second footbridge follows shortly afterwards before the slog continues. The thin old chap who ran past earlier passes by me again, now heading down and looking a touch crestfallen. Running up Ben Nevis was perhaps a tad optimistic for all but the very fittest. That being said – I feel both sympathy for the fellow and a fresh slice of foreboding for myself. Another one bites the dust.

The stony path now begins to curve round the mountain and goosebumps start to appear as I climb up above the valley of the Red Burn. I'm now starting to get to heights that I'm unaccustomed too. My experience of mountain hiking is similar to that of snow hiking: an enthusiastic novice. I've walked Snowdon in Wales as well as Pen-Y-Fan and various others across the Black Mountains and Brecon Beacons but Ben Nevis dwarfs all of these. I'm not yet as high as the peaks of some of those of course, but it's about more than just height somehow. More relevant than it being the biggest mountain in the UK at this moment is that it's the biggest in the highlands. The scale and grandeur of this brutally beautiful landscape is mind-blowing at ground level – from up here it's enough to make history's finest poets despair at the inadequacy of the written word. Or something like that... It's very nice at any rate.

The path is a ledge on the mountainside as the crowds continue to thin. We're now just beyond the point at which the last of the unprepared give up the ghost and head for home. Looking around me now there is no sign of families in jeans, or large chaps in Metallica t-shirts. All of a sudden yours truly is part of a tired looking minority not carrying walking poles or wearing shiny sunglasses. I reach the welcoming plateau beside Loch Meall an t-Suidhe where I join the groups of people taking the opportunity for a well-earned breather. I reach into the backpack for a much-needed hit of Mars Bar energy. I'm thinking I must have broken the back of the thing by now... I've been climbing for somewhere in the region of an ice age after all. I'm now up in the clouds and the temperature is dropping so one would assume another hour or so ought to do it. I decide to confirm this by consulting Mr B. He delivers the news that I'm just shy of the halfway point with a lack of bedside manner that frankly appals me. I place him back in The

Albatross and regret my decision not to leave the blaggard in a broom cupboard with the cursed tent and my smelly pants.

As I munch on the old MB I look over the attractive, if slightly ghostly, mini-loch - or Lochan as we've learnt that they're called of course, dear reader. The water and indeed the surrounding landscape have a lifeless quiet about them. Just then a group of teenagers escorted by an enthusiastic-looking adult figure plonk themselves beside me. The adult figure; a tall balding fellow with a definite Akela vibe about him, proceeds to take a roll call and make sure that none amongst their number are feeling faint and whatnot. These are not fully-fledged teenagers but rather they inhabit that no-mans-land between childhood and adolescence – something in the region of twelve or thirteen years old I would suppose (although as I've already pointed out I'm not the best at determining this kind of thing). As such they've yet to reach the 'everything's rubbish and the whole world hates me' stage of life and are all incredibly chipper. Completely unfazed by their surroundings and not a tired limb between them – save for those of the Akela. He smiles at me and sits down.

'This seemed like a good idea at the time,' he says.

I smile back at him and we chat for a few minutes. They are in fact on an after-school club outing. This surprises me a touch as my own school outings tended to involve trips to country parks or petting zoos – usually incorporating some form of child-labour wherein we'd all end up building a wall or planting trees or some such arduous endeavour. No mountain climbing involved as I recall. The fellow is an all-round good egg who, despite his jokes to the contrary, is clearly enjoying the experience at least as much as his exuberant charges.

I cross paths with the after-schoolers several more times over the next hour or so as we stop for rests at slightly different intervals. I'm passing many of the same faces over and over again in fact. As with much of the last week or so I'm struck by

147

the variety of different languages being spoken around me. I briefly wonder if I'll see Clara and Henri again... But I suppose they're effectively a day behind me now and will most likely be climbing the grand old summit tomorrow. I've also kept an eye out for the chaps I met yesterday – although now that I understand the sheer volume of people climbing the mountain at any one time, I realise there was never really any chance of bumping into them again. Nevertheless I'm once again struck by the sense of camaraderie that this trail continues to radiate. The breaking down of cultural or indeed any other barriers. For a short spell we're all as one, in search of the same ends. Out here we're all the children of the West Highland Way.

There are a few sharp turns as the path is rerouted away from weather-beaten old tracks that are no longer safe to use. The increasing number of screes that I'm passing is further evidence of this erosion. My leg muscles are now aching a good deal – but the continued drop in temperature provides adequate encouragement to keep climbing. There are frequent breaks in the clouds that reveal views below that are simply breathtaking. Fleeting glimpses of savage mountain vistas, all the more dramatic when seen from above. Staggering panoramas taking in Glen Nevis and the surrounding wilderness. The path is becoming rougher and much more challenging. Then it begins to wildly turn left then right – in increasingly wide zigzags as the gradient steepens yet further still. These striking and somewhat soul-destroying zigs and zags will eventually lead me all the way to the summit.

The cloud cover means that the end is never in sight and the relentlessness and repetitiveness of the task begins to take on an unreal quality. I feel as though there's never been a time when I wasn't exhaustedly climbing this mountain. I briefly consider that I might be dreaming. Perhaps I'm still asleep in a hotel room a few miles outside of Fort William. The continued spectacular views when the clouds break rid me of this notion however. My dreaming subconscious couldn't hope to conjure up such images. In fact, dear reader, my dreams are legendarily boring. I jest not - I once had a detailed and vivid dream about being given a guided tour round a factory where they manufacture Benecol health drinks. Seriously – I remember it well. I was shown large vats of yoghurty liquid being slowly stirred with giant spoons by men in white overalls. I was treated to a long talk on the printing machine that created the bottle labels and even shown round the canteen. No bearing on reality whatsoever of course but thoroughly detailed. I know time moves differently in a dream but the whole thing felt as though it lasted somewhere in the region of the full eight hours. When you start the day with a sense of such utter boredom how on earth can you realistically be expected to achieve anything of note? Anyway – what was I saying?

Perhaps it's the altitude causing me to go a touch peculiar. I decide to take another brief rest stop and pick a spot where the clouds part so that I temporarily get to gawp at more of those incredible views whilst I recuperate. As I trawl ever upwards the casualties that litter either side of the path increase in volume. I recognise many faces from earlier in the climb and offer a few words of encouragement as I pass by. I pass a young chap crying his eyes out being consoled by his parents. Another woman sits with her head in her hands, her backpack thrown to the floor behind her. It's all starting to get a bit tough on the old spirits when the after-schoolers appear up ahead, taking a breather and laughing merrily as though out for a Sunday stroll.

'Nearly there,' Akela says, patting me on the back with a smile.

'Define "nearly",' I reply wearily, but also smiling. A while later I reach the head of the infamous Five Finger Gully. A deadly sheer drop over the cliff edge, that's almost obscured by the deceptive gradient leading up to it. Numerous lives have been lost here over the years and in the still, lifeless and increasingly foggy landscape of the mountain, it's easy enough to imagine that the ghosts of those lost souls are not too far away. The clouds are thickening and I sense that there'll be no more majestic views until the descent back down. I'm now almost certain that there is no summit to this mountain and that one simply climbs until one can climb no longer and then turns around in an accepting defeat. It's then that a wondrous thing starts to happen: The folks passing by in the opposite direction also start enthusiastically saying, 'Nearly there!' Enough of them, in fact, that I begin to believe it might just be true.

Eventually the gradient begins to lessen and the talk around me is that we have reached the beginning of the summit's plateau. The conditions are now total whiteout and I can see no more than a few feet in either direction. The wind has increased dramatically as well and provides a wall of noise that blocks out all other sound. I'm hit by the sudden and irrational idea that whoever's at the front of this endless line of ramblers might not know where they're going and lead us all over the edge of a cliff. Not being able to see or hear anything we'll all just wander off the edge one after the other. The constant stream of people coming in the other direction calms the nerves in this regard. I'm also suddenly soaking wet. The moisture in the air is now so dense that it's dripping off me as though I've been out walking in the driving rain all day.

As I'm no longer climbing the cold has hit me and I'm shivering as I walk on through the spectral fog. I pass a young chap wearing only a t-shirt and shorts, shivering uncontrollably. I consider offering up some clothing before remembering that my entire wardrobe currently resides in a broom cupboard in the Premier Inn. I ask him if he's OK at any rate and he confirms, through chattering teeth, that he's fine and that his girlfriend will soon be appearing with an overcoat.

Where she'll be appearing from exactly I never find out... I've got a summit to stand heroically atop. The minutes continue to roll past as I blindly walk onwards and I begin to think I must have missed it. Then the cairns start to appear through the fog.

There's heaps of them, all vying for attention, each one masquerading as the true summit.

Eventually I reach the trig point and the highest point of the United Kingdom. I stand in the wet and icy cold, suddenly not shivering anymore as a feeling of pride wells up inside of me. I puff the old chest out and do my best to assume a gallant pose. It takes a while for the sensation to land – perhaps because I can't actually see anything – but when it does it's a jolly satisfactory one. The kind of triumph one feels when winning the egg and spoon race at Barnham Count Primary school's annual sports day. This is followed by an uplifting sense of joy. Like when you're standing arm in arm with your baby brother watching Carter USM's final ever gig at the Brixton Academy and singing along tearfully with three thousand other drunken warriors. Or the first time you try one of Tasha's mum's aubergine pakoras.

After a few minutes the cold penetrates its way through my sense of achievement and I feel the need to get moving again. I begin to wander back along the path the way I came, taking a brief detour to investigate the remains of an old meteorological observatory. I can't even begin to fathom the logistics of either building or operating such an establishment up here, dear reader. I trudge on through the mist until eventually, a good deal of time later, I reach the end of the plateau and begin the descent proper. I'm now a member of the smug-faced descending party, passing the continued stream of fatigued folks nearing the end of their climbs.

Like thousands – or hundreds of thousands - before me, I begin to dish out the well-intended messages of encouragement. 'Nearly there.' 'Not long to go now.' 'You can do it!' I even give one fellow a spontaneous and hearty pat on the back as he puffs his way past. This selfless gesture is met with an expression suggesting that, were it not for the fact that he's currently more exhausted than any human being has ever been in the history of human beings, he would pick me up and throw me over the cliff edge, ensuring in the process that no other unsuspecting climber will ever be subjected to my nauseating plaudits. This aside, the spirit of camaraderie is strong as I begin to negotiate my way back down the zigzag section of the path. I'm passed early on by the after-schoolers, who are practically skipping down the mountain. I also pass the woman I'd observed earlier sitting with her head in her hands. She's now striding determinedly onwards and approaching the end of the ascent. I decide against dishing out a second hearty pat on the back… But internally I'm cheering her on as though she were Mo Farah rounding the final bend.

It doesn't take long for the last of the excitement and adrenaline regards reaching the summit to wear off and for cruel realisation to hit home. Rather than the hard work being over and done with I have in fact now got hours of steep and relentless descent ahead of me. Funny the things you forget, eh? I'm distracted from this early onset of despair by a chap tentatively approaching me with a notably distressed look on his face.

'Excuse me, my friend. I'm really sorry to bother you, but do you by any chance have any food on you that I could buy off you? I'm afraid we've come up here a bit unprepared.' He looks back towards a girl sitting on a nearby rock, looking painfully embarrassed. The couple are dressed for… Well, let's just say not really for mountain climbing and leave it at that. They've embarked on the climb without bringing any food or water along and are now both in the midst of a full-on sugar crash. They're tired, blistered and broken. Enter your heroic narrator with a big sack full of Mars Bars to save the day. I hand over four of the aforementioned treats with pleasure. Despite my protestations the fellow absolutely insists on paying me for them... They're both quite obviously mortified to be having to ask for assistance in this manner and I do my level best to assure them there's really no need to worry about it.

I consider giving them a detailed run through of the mistakes I've made during this week alone, to make them feel better. I ultimately decide against this however. I'm rather partial to the idea of forever remaining in their minds the mysterious adventurer with the dashed impressive moustache who appeared through the mist near the summit of Ben Nevis to save their lives on that fateful day. I wonder briefly if I should formally introduce myself, just in case they want to name any of their children after me.

This incredible act of heroism succeeds in fending off the tiredness for a short while longer as I get going once more. As I look about me I realise that at this point during the ascent I had yet to reach the foggy whiteout stage of proceedings. The fog or mist... or cloud; whatever the bally thing is, is spreading down the mountain at a quicker rate than my weary legs can carry me. The effect is as though someone has taken an eraser to the view and simply rubbed it all out. Then I reach a small section that they must've missed and a grand vista is briefly visible below. I stop and snap a couple of selfies, doing my very best to smile and hide the growing exhaustion. I'm conscious that the pics I took atop the summit could really have been taken anywhere, showing as they do a red-faced and dripping wet S. Reynolds standing in front of a plain white backdrop. As I continue the remorseless descent these glimpsed visions through the white become more frequent until, eventually, I find myself below the cloud cover once more.

After a few more millennia have passed I reach the Flintstones steps and begin to believe that life at ground level may be more than a false memory. The endless line of climbers passing me now once again includes within its ranks scores of unsuspecting families and denim-clad holidaymakers. I pick a spot with a decent view – not a difficult task – and sit myself down with luncheon in mind. Due to my earlier heroism (and even earlier discarding of the last remaining stringy cheeses), my supply now totals two squishy Mars Bars and a couple of swigs of water. I consume this veritable feast greedily and allow myself ten minutes to gaze out at - what I suddenly realise will be - my last grand Highland panorama. The dual streams of passing climbers and accompanying hum of chatter fade into a distant fuzz of blurred colour and sound, as I focus on the vast ancient valley beyond. The mountain tops are obscured by rolling grey and purple clouds as below their sides are scorched and scarred by glowing white pathways and plantations of darkest green.

Afternoon

I tear myself reluctantly away from the view in order to face the final big push down the mountainside. I find myself mumbling the mantra: 'You put your left foot down then your right foot down... All your feet down but you'll never reach the ground.' To the tune of the hokey-cokey. I don't have the strength to put the brakes on this particular maddening mental loop and so I decide to just go with it; repeating it endlessly as the time rolls by and my leg muscles slowly turn to jelly. Then – somehow – just before my brain and body finally become complete mush – I reach the bottom of the mountain. I drag my feet in a zombie-like motion across the futuristic footbridge and back into the visitor's centre car park.

To my amazement there still appear to be hundreds of people preparing for the off, in the manner that there were when I last stood here, a lifetime ago. My brain struggles to comprehend how this can be possible as there surely isn't nearly enough daylight remaining to complete the climb now? Then I glance at my phone to see that it's only mid-afternoon. 'Nonsense - you ridiculous machine,' I declare, I hope internally but I really can't be certain at this point. I wander vacantly into a small hut selling maps, climbing gear, Ben Nevis memorabilia and suchlike. I scan the four walls and see with pure unadulterated joy that they sell Irn-Bru. Never has my need for the luminous sugary liquid been so great. I carry it like a trophy to a patch of nearby grass and plonk myself down, discarding the almost empty Albatross in the process.

The liquid bubble-gum combined with around fifteen minutes of rest seem to do the trick. I drag myself to my feet and begin the slog of a few miles back to Fort William. Shortly after leaving the visitor's centre, as I'm ambling along the roadside, my phone rings and I look down to see that Pops is calling me. He's eager to hear how the climb went and he and Jane both offer their congratulations regards completing the trail. They also make fun of me – if you can believe it, dear reader - regards the whole Tent-gate, getting bitten and bringing a beauty product instead of insect repellent to Scotland in the height of midge season *thing*. Being a generous and forgiving chap I decide to focus on the congratulatory elements of the call. I do my best to explain the experience of climbing Ben Nevis;

'When you think you must be nearly at the top you're actually half way. Then when you finally give up on the idea of ever reaching the top... That's when you're nearly there.'

'Could we do it?' Pops enquires.

'Yes, of course,' I reply. It's true - and not just because Pops is himself an experienced hiker. On a day like today anyone could do it, as long as they've prepared, dressed appropriately and brought adequate supplies with them. On a day like today, the truth is of course that you don't actually 'climb' Ben Nevis... you walk up it. That being said, as I'm relaying the adventure to my attentive audience the swell of pride I experienced at the summit makes a welcome encore.

Once I've said my goodbyes to Pops and Jane I realise that whilst I've been chatting away I've walked a good mile of the journey back to Fort William already. With this in mind I decide to use the rest of the stroll to make the final calls of the trip to my remaining loved ones. I re-emphasize the whole 'walking not climbing' up Ben Nevis situation to old Mumsy whilst being careful to leave out the dangerously deteriorating standard of my daily diet.

'And Dennis wants to know if you've tried any good whiskies?'

You won't be surprised to hear that in the version of events Tasha gets I'm most definitely 'climbing' the mountain. I'm also 'navigating' my way around the deadly Five Finger Gully – and it was pretty hairy there for a while let me tell you. Then of course there was the whole rescue mission to save the lives of the couple stranded on the mountain with no food or water. During the call to my brother Mark we mostly talk about the disturbing recent rumours suggesting that Peter Capaldi won't be reprising his role as Doctor Who next year (be quiet, we're cool). Lastly - I take the opportunity to message and send some pics to a few friends who've been asking for updates during the course of the week. This includes my some-time walking companion Mickey B; the teetotal vegetarian from Barnsley. He messages me back to ask:

'Did you actually use your tent this time?'

When I finally arrive back in Fort William I check into the hotel and collect my things from the broom cupboard before trudging up to my room for a siesta and a bubble bath. On my way to the room I pass a girl in hiking gear in the corridor. She looks me up and down and then laughs

'Have you just finished the West Highland Way?' she says, as a few more girls emerge from nearby doorways to join her.

'Yeah I have,' I reply sleepily.

'Thought so, you look how I feel. We've just finished it as well.'

In the last comradely encounter of the journey I chat to the young group of fellow ramblers about our respective experiences of this magical trail, before retiring to my room.

The room is spookily identical to the one I stayed in a week ago in Milngavie. I eventually decide this gives the trip a pleasing circularity and duly set about running the aforementioned bubble bath.

Well, there you have it, dear reader: The West Highland Way, done and dusted. So what was the moral of the story? Well... There wasn't one... It's a hiking book. Well then, what did we learn? Well... Um... Oh OK, how about that although the folklore surrounding Avon Skin So Soft is absolutely true (and I'd wholeheartedly recommend it to help keep those pesky midges at bay – good shout A. Walker), you will definitely need to pack insect repellent as well. Definitely. Also – stringy cheeses. Delicious processed snacks? Yes. Adequate main luncheon ingredient? No. Irn-Bru is great. I never did learn what a neep or a tattie was, did I? Hang on I'll consult the phone... Turnips or swedes and potatoes. Hmm, I mean these aren't exactly game-changing learnings, are they?

Well... Um... Crikey... OK, how about this as a moral of the story? Walk more. Yes, that's it - everyone should walk more... Spend more time walking, everyone. That's the message. Or rather, if walking's not your thing then find out what your thing is and do *that* more. 'Easy for you to say, Mr reduced-working-hours with your fancy-pants alternative lifestyle, no children and stupid face.' Well... A fair shout perhaps. Then again perhaps not. I'm childless of course – and thus have no financial dependants. If that were not the case then the life choices I've made recently may not have been possible. They certainly haven't felt like easy choices though. I'm poorer than I've ever been for a kick-off: my pants have no elastic, my new jeans are my baby brother's hand-me-downs and my car has a billion miles on the clock. (I swear that when I start the engine of a morning I can actually hear it crying out, 'Please… Please just let me die'.) But in all honesty, I could not care less. It's just stuff. As Tasha would put it; first world problems. Everyone is different – you may like stuff. In which case definitely don't go part-time at work… That would be stupid. Just ask yourself what's important to *you* is all I'm saying. That's the nub of the thing. Ask yourself want you want, what you need. Never stop asking – don't just get carried along the wrong path because it's easier than changing your mind. We only get one go… Oh, listen to me. Who on Earth does this idiot think he is? I know, I know. Whatever. I guess I'll leave it at this: We're all different yes? With different passions, ideals and needs. So how come most of us are living exactly the same lifestyle? Work. Sleep. Repeat.

Epilogue

Only a week when all is said and done. But then a week on the West Highland Way doesn't pass by in the same way as a week in the real world. I've seen the sunrise over the Bridge of Orchy, witnessed it fall across the ghostly still waters of Loch Lomond. I've watched the vast storm clouds gather and engulf the mighty Ben More. I've conquered the Devil's Staircase and felt the wildness that courses through the veins of the red stag that run on Rannoch Moor.

I've stood atop our islands summit and felt its icy winds howling through my bones. There is poetry in this place. Moments I will keep with me for the rest of my days. Moments that will sustain me through the weeks and months that follow, as the dull familiarity of routine and responsibility slowly dampen the flame of Highland spirit that stowed away inside my soul.

A trail in the truest and noblest sense. Its popularity is both justified and irrelevant. It matters not how well-trodden the path, or how many other people you pass along the way. They are kindred spirits that seek, and always find, the release that this wilderness brings. The solace and perspective that this ancient and remote landscape gladly yields to each and every traveller who is willing to give up something of themselves in return. And give it up we always do, for how can we not? We arrive as shop assistants, students and office workers – but we leave as the wild men and women of the West Highland Way.

So, even as I now sit - as all who shared that path with me now doubtless do - in front of glaring monitors in air-conditioned rooms, I smile in the knowledge that hundreds of miles away in a better place than this, there are shop assistants, students and office workers howling silently at the moon. The wild men and women of the West Highland Way.

Rejected Book Titles:

- **Just Off For A Dauner**

(My last book was called Just Off For A Walk... As explained earlier, Dauner is Scottish for walk. I still like this one... but everyone I suggested it to pleaded with me not to call the book this... so blame them if you like it too.)

- **Just Away For A Wee Dauner**

(As above really, this is the full saying.)

- **The Nomad En Suite**

(Still my favourite – again other people didn't like it so much... they thought it was too obscure and that nobody would buy the book. They could be right... I reserve the right to use this next time though.)

A few words I definitely used too many times due to general lack of intelligence:

Wilderness
Remote
Desolate
Vista
Irn-Bru
Shimmering
Vast

Situation Appropriate
Internal Theme Tunes

- **Quantum Leap:** Best for work-related scenarios. If you're being given instructions you've no chance of grasping – why panic when you could be thinking about Scott Bakula instead?

- **A Question of Sport:** Geology/geography related scenarios. Someone is speaking to you about rocks but you don't know your granite from your basalt? Don't worry just crank up the QoS them tune inside your head and imagine Sue Barker laughing heartily as Tuffers mimes riding a horse in the Grand National. Oh, Tuffers!

- **Police Academy:** Unwanted learning scenarios. Did you accidently express interest in something (a piece of furniture or a painting, perhaps?) and now someone is giving you a potted history you simply don't have the attention span to digest? No problem – do you think Mahoney or High Tower wasted time learning about stuff? Of course not.

- **Doctor Who:** Science (self-explanatory – although it works best if it's the 80's version).

- **Jamie and the Magic Torch:** Political discussions. Are your peers waxing lyrical about the latest parliamentary developments? With this punchy number cranked up in your cranium you won't hear a word.

- **Count Duckula:** Anything to do with cars. Is your Pops trying to explain what a driveshaft does? Is a close chum attempting to talk you through the basics of piston rods, rings or heads? *In the heart of Transylvania, in the vampire hall of fame yeah...*

Lightning Source UK Ltd.
Milton Keynes UK
UKHW020950090321
380036UK00009B/337